THE RIGHT TO VOTE

THE
RIGHT
TO
VOTE

By Bill Severn

Ives Washburn, Inc.
New York

THE RIGHT TO VOTE

LIBRARY OF CONGRESS CATALOG CARD NUMBER: 76-165010

MANUFACTURED IN THE UNITED STATES OF AMERICA

DESIGNED BY SOPHIE ADLER

1

"Young people are highly skeptical, often cynical about our institutions. But youth cares. Care as it may, it seems powerless to affect the things that concern it most. What can the 18-year-old do about a war which seems unbearably cruel, starvation . . . malnutrition . . . racial discrimination, the threat of nuclear holocaust, injustice, bulldozers leveling the last park where you can sit under a tree, schools that ignore needs and drill in the seemingly irrelevant, massive pollution of air, water, noise, anxiety and violence—threats to the environment that almost suffocate?"

Former Attorney General Ramsey Clark asked the question at a Senate committee hearing in 1970, when he appeared as one of the many witnesses urging congress to grant 18-year-olds the right to vote.

"Youth is excluded from the initial step in the decision process devised by our system of government—the vote," he said. "We must start our young people voting during their last year of high school. We must involve them in our system and then work to keep them in meaningful participation in the system. If we do, the system will work. The fault is not with the system, but with ourselves. The 18-year-old vote is an essential element in the vitalization of American democracy."

By 1971 the right to vote had become a reality for young Americans of eighteen. Youth finally had gained some political power "to affect the things that concern it most," and the nation had gained a broadened democracy.

America once was a place where only the landed gentry voted and where the common man who owned no property or who lacked a fixed amount of wealth couldn't vote at all. The early American had no say in choosing a president because that choice was made for him by members of state legislatures. For much longer, senators were chosen in the same way, not by direct vote of the people. When a man did vote he had to declare his choice in public, not by secret ballot. Even in later years America was a country where more than half the people couldn't vote because they were female, or because they were black, or because they were young.

In their long struggle to increase the right to vote, more power for the people is what Americans have been gaining since the nation began. From colonial days to the present, the battle for the right to vote has been a people's fight all the way. Although the Declaration of Independence held out the promise of a government that would derive its powers "from the consent of the governed," it was the people who fought, step by step, to make good that promise.

The framers of the constitution and the founders of almost every state carefully restricted voting to keep the new republic from becoming a people's democracy. But gradually the people won power and went on winning it, until they had perhaps greater voting rights than the people of any other major nation.

Property requirements for voting gave way to voting rights for taxpayers and then to ballot privileges for nearly all white male adults. The secret ballot was won. People won the right to vote for presidential electors. Senators were chosen by direct vote. Women were allowed to vote. Blacks were given the promise if not always the reality of voting, and that fight went on through a century. Many voting reforms are still needed, but the victory of young people in gaining the right to vote has brought the nation close to the goal of truly universal suffrage.

The American "system" is government by peaceable argument. People take sides, debate and air their views, and then vote to reach a decision. That doesn't mean that the argument is over or that the decision is final. It means the voters have agreed to abide by the decision of the majority for a specified length of time, or until the next vote is taken. The winners and losers come to a compromise which lets government go on functioning, because if government had to wait for everybody to agree it couldn't act at all.

Voters make certain rules for the contests called voting laws and rights. They agree in advance to accept the results of the voting, at least temporarily. What they don't agree to do is to quit arguing, because if they did there would be no democracy. When the next vote comes around, the majority may decide to keep things as they are, but it also may vote to change them.

In the United States, "government by the consent of the

governed" never means full consent. At any time, up to almost half the voters may be opposed to those who happen to be in power or may be against what is being done. What the minority does consent to accept is the operation of a system in which argument, persuasion and votes may, at any time, change or at least influence the majority.

Even the smallest minority, by actively participating, has some influence, and often it is much greater than its numbers would indicate. Democracy's vitality lies in the fact that all its decisions are always subject to change, as the views of the people and the conditions of life within the country change. Voting is a means of change.

By constantly enlarging the number of eligible voters, Americans have enlarged the whole basis of consent. They have created not only a much larger but a different majority, so that a voting decision gradually has come to mean one in which all classes of people have some voice.

But the struggle for voting rights has involved more than merely adding numbers of people to the lists of those eligible. Just as vital have been the battles for freedom of choice. In totalitarian countries people often have the right to vote but it is an empty right because they go to the polls merely to confirm the choice already made for them by a dictator or by a self-appointed power group. Americans have freedom to choose among candidates and issues, but they also have had to fight for a greater voice in the basic process of nominating candidates and to bring important issues before the voters.

Nominations of candidates were once made by members of congress, by state legislatures, then by state conventions, and with the growth of the political party system by primary elections and national conventions. Young people in recent years, even before the 18-year-old vote, have had a dramatic effect upon primary elections. By involving themselves in political action at its roots, when the decisions about presenting candidates and issues are really made, long before election day, they have helped to enlarge the freedom of choice.

Future young voters, working within the parties, still have a battle ahead of them to increase freedom of choice and to influence issues in national conventions, and to see to it that their own voting rights and those of others are fully granted, according to law. Behind them they have the heritage of two hundred years in which Americans have been hammering out for themselves the right to vote.

2

From ENGLAND, colonial America inherited representative government, but also voting discrimination, so that the people themselves had to fight through the years for equal voting rights. It also inherited a system in which voting qualifications greatly varied from one area to another, with no uniformity.

Before the colonial period ended British subjects in America had come to think about elections as Britons did at home and in nearly all the colonies voting for members of legislatures was restricted to a middle and upper class. Virginia, which started its colonial years with free manhood suffrage, ended them with more voting restrictions of one kind or another than any of the other colonies.

American colonists, although loyal to the monarchy, rejected the divine right of kings and insisted that the people must have a vote in running their affairs, but not all the people. They substituted what became almost a "divine" right of property.

The voter usually had to be a freeholder: the lifetime owner of property by outright grant or unlimited purchase, and it had to be a piece of property of specified value, not just a scrap of land. Some American colonies adopted the British yardstick of land that produced a minimum income of forty shillings a year and others set different values to define a freeholder. Values were changed frequently so as to restrict the vote to those considered the "better class" of citizens.

As cities grew and land became scarcer, ways were found to include substantial townsmen among the voters by accepting not only freeholders but also those who possessed some equivalent in personal property. A man's right to vote might be determined by his furniture or personal belongings or by the goods, animals or slaves he owned, which had to be worth a certain minimum amount.

Other restrictions gradually were added, sometimes to deny the vote on the basis of race, religion or the sort of work a man did. Kept from voting were "drifters" and temporary residents, those beneath the age of twenty-one, and all females, who were not expected to take part in man's affairs. But property was the main qualification, rather than character, beliefs, nationality or length of residence. His right to vote was measured largely in terms of his material belongings and mainly in terms of land.

Among the colonies, Maryland deprived former servants of the vote at about the same time. In its first years of colonial government Maryland had been more liberal than most colonies, granting them not only the right to vote but the right to become elected members of its assembly. But in 1670 the sheriffs of Maryland were ordered not to accept any man as a voter unless he was the freeholder of fifty acres of land or had a personal estate of forty pounds sterling.

South Carolina began with laws that allowed almost any adult Protestant white man to vote, but by 1719 apprentices and sailors were excluded and other restrictions gradually were added until by 1759 a voter had to own one hundred acres of land or be a substantial taxpayer. Power was concentrated in the hands of the wealthy even more by requiring those elected as representatives to own five hundred acres of land and ten slaves or to have personal property worth one thousand pounds.

Prosperous New York colonists complained that even the traditional English standard of the forty-shilling freeholder, which they tried to maintain at first, was too liberal because "men of no great figure, tailors and others in mean conditions" were not only voting but also getting elected to office. In 1699 New York raised the value of the required freehold from forty shillings to forty pounds. In New Jersey by 1725 the voter had to be a freeholder and worth fifty pounds. Pennsylvania and Delaware also required a personal estate or certain amount of land as a voting qualification.

Some New England colonies started by restricting the vote to members of a specified church but gradually lifted religious barriers and substituted those of land or money. In Rhode Island a freeholder's eldest son could inherit the right to vote just as he inherited his father's property. When Georgia, last of the thirteen original colonies, shifted from semi-military government to a representative assembly in 1752, it also imposed a voting requirement of at least fifty acres of land.

It wasn't only the desire of the wealthy to keep control of the law-making process that made property the measure of the right to vote. England often included such qualifications in its instructions to colonial governments and they were readily accepted by colonial leaders because it was the prevailing political thought in almost all of Europe that property owners were the backbone of both society and the state.

Men who owned land shared a common interest in maintaining law and order and good government. They paid the bulk of public taxes, had the education and leisure to interest themselves in public affairs, and the proper standing in the community to command the respect of others. Many colonies started as business ventures to develop settlement and trade, and so it was thought that owning property was the equivalent of owning stock in a corporation entitling the stockholder to vote.

Voting restrictions were considered necessary to protect the "good of the state" from relatively poor and uneducated men who, because they owned no property, might vote recklessly, swayed by personal need and desire, or influenced by others who could dominate them because of their property. The growth in size of the colonies and the increasing arrival of "strangers" also strengthened restrictions.

In an age when even limited democracy was new, hardly anybody believed that everybody should vote. However, despite the seemingly tight restrictions, a fairly large number of men did manage to do so. In some colonies the electorate amounted to half the adult males or more.

Benjamin Franklin once remarked with patriotic hyperbole that every New Englander was a freeholder but for the average middle class American land was not too difficult to obtain and many had enough to satisfy freehold requirements. To be an accepted freeholder often was easier than to meet personal property tests for voting, but even those were likely to depend on local conditions. A man who owned a horse, a few cows, tools of work, or almost anything at all, might convince local officials his small possessions legally qualified him as a voter.

There also was a wide gap between the suffrage laws and the enforcement of them. Many colonials were ignorant of the laws or plainly indifferent to them. In some areas the laws were openly ignored and few men of decent character, respected and liked in the community, were rejected as voters. A man's acceptance by his neighbors might be all the qualification he needed to cast his vote with theirs. But restrictions were always avaliable to deny the right to "undesirables."

As America neared the time of the Revolution only the owners of land were legally entitled to vote in seven of the thirteen colonies. Four of those seven restricted the vote according to the amount of land owned and the other three to the cash value or income from it. The other six colonies also had real estate qualifications, but allowed alternatives so that a man who owned no land could vote if his personal worth or other property amounted to from forty to fifty pounds.

Although the laws varied from colony to colony, their general intent was to keep voting in the control of prosperous adult white male Protestant property owners. Some specifically barred voting by strangers, drunks, former criminals, servants, women, Indians, Catholics, Jews and

Negroes. Free blacks were allowed to vote in some colonies but not in others.

The majority of colonial Americans approved the restrictive franchise as a system that tended to silence dissent and nonconformity and that seemed to guarantee stability and orderly government. The colonies had come through long years of experiment to reach the stage of established government and they did not encourage political diversity.

But as Americans became more aware of their grievances against the King of England they also became more politically demanding of their own governments at home. The power of the vote grew vital in the struggle leading to the life and death struggle of the Revolution, and there was a rising demand of the people for greater voting freedom.

3

AMONG THE NATION'S founding fathers few were more respected advocates of American liberty than John Adams, but one liberty he did not believe in was the right of everybody to vote. Asked for his advice in the spring of 1776 when the colonies were revolting against British rule and forming new governments of their own, Adams warned that to grant the vote to everybody would bring political disaster.

When James Sullivan, a member of the Massachusetts legislature, suggested it would be a good time to reform the voting laws, Adams answered that while "it is certain, in theory, that the only moral foundation of government is the consent of the governed," the theory should not be carried to ridiculous and impossible lengths so that "every individual of the community, old and young, male and female, as well as rich and poor, must consent, expressly, to every act of legislation."

The voting qualifications should be left as they were, Adams said, because if they were liberalized in any way people might start demanding all sorts of new voting rights. Even "women will demand a vote," he wrote, and "lads from twelve to twenty-one will think their rights not closely enough attended to; and every man who has not a farthing will demand an equal voice with any other." The result, in Adams' view, would be political chaos. To give everybody the vote would be "to confound and destroy all distinctions, and prostrate all ranks to one common level."

Along with most of America's leaders at the time of the Revolution he believed that restricting the vote to men of property was necessary because "men in general, in every society, who are wholly destitute of property, are also too little acquainted with public affairs to form a right judgment, and too dependent upon other men to have a will of their own."

But the people, if not their leaders, were aroused by the Revolution to demand liberal changes in voting laws. People became consciously aware, as never before, of the power of the vote in its direct effect on their lives and suffrage became a burning issue of public debate that produced a ferment of democracy. The Revolution was a starting point in the shift of political power from those who held office to those who elected them. It didn't accomplish that transfer of power to the people, but it began the long change.

Young men of military age led the demand for voting reform. More than others it was younger men who were denied the vote because they had not yet acquired land or belongings. In some colonies four-fifths of those in military service lacked enough property to vote. As Revolution approached they protested that if they were fit to fight for liberty they were fit to vote.

As volunteer soldiers they demanded and usually won the right to elect their own militia officers. When the Con-

tinental Congress called for the enlistment of all able-
bodied males over the age of sixteen in the summer of
1775 it recommended that all military groups should encourage them to join by letting them elect the officers who
would command them. The young soldiers of Revolution
carried that spirit of democracy over into contests for ci-
vilian voting rights.

Generally it was older men who resisted. There was genu-
ine fear among many of the older patriots that Revolution
might unleash a democracy that would turn into destruc-
tive mob rule. Still not all older men felt that way.

Among those who sided with election reformers was Benjamin Franklin, a man who grew more liberal in many ways
as he grew older. As a young man he had considered it
wrong to allow any but freeholders to vote, but as America
began to accuse Britain of taxation without representation,
Franklin became convinced that it was a two-way road. He
argued as early as 1770 that if Americans rejected the right
of Parliament to tax them without their approval they had
an equal right as taxpayers, whether they owned property
or not, to reject such a system at home. "The franchise,"
Franklin wrote, "is the common right of freemen."

There was a growing public opinion that all taxpayers
should be allowed to vote and the whole thrust of Revolution was toward increasing democracy. Men of property
and those who owned nothing rallied together around the
Liberty Trees to denounce the British with equal voice and
their grievances often included the failure of the King's
colonial governors to grant freer suffrage.

In rural gatherings held to adopt resolutions against the
British and in town and area meetings entire communities

took upon themselves the right to vote for delegates. In some colonies they also took the matter of deciding who could vote in regular elections into their own hands. Young men under voting age, tenants and others not legally entitled to vote, turned out in large numbers to cast ballots and frequently went unchallenged.

When the call was issued for the first Continental Congress to meet in Philadelphia in 1774 the problem was how to choose delegates. Leaders insisted the new congress would have no authority without the approval of colonial legislatures which represented citizens legally entitled to vote. But Britain's royal governors could not be expected to sit by while their legislatures elected delegates to what the British considered an illegal congress. Each colony solved the problem in its own way.

New Hampshire was the first of the future United States to end freehold qualifications for voting and also the first to create its own constitution. When its self-made provincial congress took over the powers of government after the collapse of British control, New Hampshire was still operating under its colonial election restrictions of 1728, which limited voting to those who owned real estate worth at least fifty pounds. Younger men and new settlers demanded equal representation in New Hampshire's provincial congress with wealthier landowners who had dominated the old colonial legislature, and in November, 1775, New Hampshire abandoned forever its freehold restrictions and granted the right to vote to "every male inhabitant . . . of twenty-one years and upwards, paying for himself a poll tax."

In Virginia there was no change in voting rights when it declared itself an independent state and adopted a new constitution in June, 1776. Virginia's historic bill of rights, the parent of all American bills of rights, declared in ringing words that "all power is vested in, and consequently derived from, the people," but there was no thought of including landless people among the voters. The new Virginia constitution kept the old colonial property restrictions intact, with a single sentence that said: "The right of suffrage in the election of members for both houses shall remain as exercised at present."

New Jersey's new provincial government, while not shifting the basis for voting from men of property to common taxpayers, did remove its freehold restrictions. It opened the vote in July, 1776, to "all inhabitants of this colony of full age who are worth fifty pounds . . . clear estate," meaning all who claimed belongings of any kind worth that much.

In Pennsylvania there was a full revolution in government. The revolutionaries overturned the old government, tore up the old voting laws, ousted rich conservatives from control, put ordinary people in power, and wrote a new constitution that created a radically new political system.

Pennsylvania's revolution was carried out with the consent of the Continental Congress and with the help of young radicals such as Tom Paine and old radicals such as Ben Franklin. Even conservative John Adams had a hand in it, although he later was horrified by the new constitution which he called "the worst that has been established in America."

Thomas Paine, whose pamphlet *Common Sense* had

spread over the colonies by 1776 by thousands of copies to influence all America with its call for an immediate declaration of independence, had made a direct attack in it against the Pennsylvania assembly. Its instructions to the delegates, he charged, had thwarted the will of the people because the assembly had been manipulated by "*a few, a very few*" political bosses who assumed the right to act "in behalf of the whole colony."

The Continental Congress was meeting in Philadelphia's State House in May, 1776, with many of its leaders determined to seek immediate American independence. By a narrow vote, the Continental Congress approved a resolution inviting all the colonies to form their own governments. Adams wrote the text of the call for governments to be formed "under the authority of the people."

Ten days later, when the Pennsylvania assembly began its session in the same building, four thousand people crowded into the State House yard for a demonstration called by the revolutionaries. Standing in a pouring rain, they heard a public reading of the Congressional resolution. Ignoring the assembly inside, the people in the yard took their own vote then and there, and unanimously approved calling a constitutional convention to create a new government for Pennsylvania.

Unanimously elected, Benjamin Franklin served as presiding officer when the convention, meeting in Philadelphia in mid-July, began to write a new Pennsylvania constitution.

Pennsylvania's people temporarily abolished the office of governor, replacing it with an elected council. Refusing to tolerate an aristocratic upper house, they also temporarily created a one-chamber legislature with all power vested in it. Most radical of all was the new suffrage law. It gave the right to vote to any man who had lived in Pennsylvania for a year, without other qualifications, if he was over twenty-one and had paid taxes.

The Pennsylvania constitution of 1776, with its underlying democratic theory that every American should have the right to vote, became a beacon for election reformers in other colonies. It had an immediate effect on the new frontier community of Vermont. Ethan Allen and his brothers, who had led the Green Mountain Boys in their battles to separate Vermont both from Britain and from New York, used a copy of the Pennsylvania constitution as a model when Vermont first declared itself an independent state in 1777.

Vermont adopted much of Pennsylvania's constitution as its own, but carried voting freedom all the way to become the first Revolutionary state to divorce both property and taxpaying from the right to vote. Every adult male was declared a voter and any man could be elected to office.

Pennsylvania's constitution also inspired a fight in Maryland for less sweeping voting reforms and Georgia was influenced by it to the extent of lifting freehold qualifications. John Adams by then thought Pennsylvania was a bad influence on other colonies and decided to publish his own *Thoughts on Government* to guide those who sought his advice in framing new state constitutions. To provide a government of checks and balances, Adams wrote, property should have its stronghold in an upper house, the people should have their voice through a lower house, and the governor should be a strong chief executive to represent the authority of the state. As far as greater voting freedom was concerned, Adams thought there should be none until America was more tranquil.

Under Adams' guidance his own state of Massachusetts adopted the most conservative of all the new constitutions, which he drafted himself. It provided for a governor elected by the people and a popularly elected house of representatives, but also for a senate proportioned according to taxable wealth instead of population. Massachusetts not only kept property restrictions on voting but increased them to limit voting rights and the right of election to office.

Many other colonies resisted all efforts to change their voting laws during the Revolutionary War years and property still remained their measure of a man's right to vote. But the people had made some important gains, and more important, they had set themselves on the long road toward democratic suffrage as a right they were determined to have.

4

MORE VOTING power for the people was not what the makers of the Constitution of the United States had in mind. The growing democracy of the common man was considered an evil to be guarded against by most of the delegates who gathered in Philadelphia in 1787 to create a new republic. They sounded many warnings that some of the state constitutions written during the Revolution had given the ordinary people too much of a direct voice in government.

"The people," Alexander Hamilton told the Constitutional Convention, "seldom judge or determine right." He thought the time had come to create a strong national government that would be largely protected from "an excess of democracy" and from the "violence and turbulence of the democratic spirit." Hamilton recommended having the nation's president and senators hold office for life instead of for short terms and he wanted them chosen indirectly by men who were lifetime owners of land.

Edmund Randolph of Virginia thought that none of the state constitutions "provided sufficient checks against the democracy." He warned that "our chief danger arises from

20

the democratic parts of our constitutions" and that "the power of government exercised by the people swallows up the other branches."

Randolph, along with others, argued that the Senate, at least, should be made a strong barrier to protect men of property against the "follies" and "evils" of the common voter. John Dickinson of Delaware agreed that the Senate should be divorced from the direct will of the people so that it would become to the United States what the House of Lords was to England.

James Madison's view was that "our government ought to secure the permanent interests of the country against innovation" and that the constitution should "protect the minority of the opulent against the majority." He pointed out that in England the elections were not open to all classes of people because if everybody could vote "the property of the landed proprietors would be insecure."

Madison foresaw a growing nation in which there would be more laborers than landowners and feared the industrial poor might overbalance future elections. Already there were enough "symptoms of a leveling spirit," he said, "to give notice of the future danger" of political equality.

The framers of the constitution finally decided both the presidency and the Senate should be protected from a direct vote of the people. The president was to be chosen by electors who would be appointed by state legislatures. Each legislature also would choose two senators so that the states, regardless of their population, would be equally represented in the aristocratic upper house.

Some of the convention delegates thought members of the lower house also should be chosen by the state legislatures instead of by the people. Roger Sherman of Connecticut argued that the people directly "should have as little to do as may be about the government" because they were "constantly liable to be misled."

But the majority decided it was a risk the new nation would have to take and that representatives ought to be elected by "the People of the several states." As Virginian George Mason put it, the House of Representatives should be "the grand depository of the democratic principle of the government . . . so to speak, our House of Commons."

That still left the question of *which* people should be granted the right to vote for representatives. Members of the British House of Commons were elected by corporations and forty-shilling freeholders, but Americans had won more liberal voting rights in some of the states. Every state had its own voting qualifications and voters in state elections would demand those rights when it came to electing national representatives.

The problem was turned over to the Committee of Detail, whose members found no way to write national voting requirements that would not deny the vote to some of those who already had it or extend the vote to those whose rights were still limited. The committee suggested that the whole matter of voting rights should be left to the individual states. Any man qualified to vote for members of the lower house of the legislature of his particular state should have the right to vote for a member of the national House of Representatives.

When that plan was put before the whole Constitutional Convention for debate it came under heavy attack by delegates who wanted to revive the freeholder qualifications of America's colonial days. Wealthy and aristocratic Gouverneur Morris, a former New Yorker but then living in Philadelphia, moved to throw out the committee report and substitute wording that would restrict the right to vote to freeholders. Another Pennsylvania delegate, Thomas Fitzsimmons, promptly seconded the motion to write into the basic law of the land a rule that only men of property could vote for representatives.

John Dickinson of Delaware also argued that freeholders should be the only ones allowed to vote because they were the nation's "best guardians of liberty" who would defend it against reckless voting by "those multitudes without property and without principle." James Madison sided with those who wanted to restrict the vote. "In future times a great majority of people will not only be without land but any other sort of property," Madison said, and "the rights of property and the public liberty will not be secure in their hands."

The restrictionists, however, fought a losing battle. It was one they had already lost in the states where voting changes were eliminating freehold qualifications. Against the arguments of those who tried to write the old freehold restrictions into the constitution, other delegates rose to support the new voting freedoms and to warn that the American people would not back a national government that tried to take away voting rights.

Suffrage was "a tender point" with the people, Oliver Ellsworth of Connecticut reminded the constitution makers. "The people," he said, "will not readily subscribe to the national constitution if it should subject them to be disfranchised." Pierce Butler of South Carolina declared, "There is no right of which the people are more jealous than that of suffrage."

The Revolution had been largely fought and won by "the lower class of citizens," Benjamin Franklin said, in a stirring defense of the democratic right to vote. "If denied the right of suffrage it would debase their spirit and detach them from the interests of the country." The love of country flourished where the common people had the vote and it withered where they were denied it, Franklin said, and the future strength of America might well depend upon suffrage freedoms. It was of vital importance, he urged, "that we should not depress the virtue and public spirit of our common people."

After less than a day the constitutional debate over suffrage was brought to an end by those who made it clear that the people had broken the old freehold pattern in the states and had gained voting rights they were not about to surrender to the new national government. When the vote was taken the delegates, by a large majority, rejected the attempt to write freehold restrictions into the constitution and accepted the idea that each state should determine the qualifications of its voters. The wording finally made part of the constitution was:

"The House of Representatives shall be composed of members chosen every second year by the people of the several states, and the electors in each state shall have the qualifications requisite for electors of the most numerous branch of the State Legislature."

However, the new constitution did not provide for the direct election by the people of any national officers except members of the House of Representatives. It specifically protected the Senate from the immediate influence of the voters. "The Senate of the United States shall be composed of two Senators from each state," it said, "chosen by the Legislature thereof, for six years . . ."

There was another provision of the constitution that was to become increasingly important in the years ahead. While each state could decide who was eligible to vote, congress was given the ultimate power to regulate the way in which elections were held. The constitution said, "The times, places and manner of holding elections for Senators and Representatives, shall be prescribed in each state by the Legislature thereof, but—" and the "but" was a big one— "the Congress may at any time by law make or alter such regulations . . ."

Congress could not tell the states *who* was to vote, but it could tell them *how* the voting was to be conducted. It could not grant anybody the right to vote but it could insist that all voters who were qualified by a state had to be treated equally and it could control the way in which states organized their election systems. The constitution also gave to each house of congress the right to "be the judge of the elections, returns and qualifications of its own members."

By permitting each state to determine who should be allowed to vote in national as well as in state elections the Founding Fathers left the states free to impose whatever requirements they wished, or even to disfranchise citizens because of race, color, age, sex, or for any other reason. The lack of a uniform national election law meant the qualifications of voters would vary from state to state according to where a voter happened to live. It also meant that the battles for voting rights would have to be fought out state by state through the years to come.

The framers of the constitution had never seriously considered liberalizing voting rights. The debate had been over whether to restrict them even more or leave them as they were. Most delegates to the Constitutional Convention expected the states to keep the restrictions then in force to protect men of property from the "dangers" of democracy.

But democracy was on the rise everywhere in the new United States. In the older states, as population grew, more people sought the right to vote. On the frontiers, where new states were forming, many men considered it only right that their neighbors should be allowed to vote whether they had property or not. Gradually some of the old restrictions were broken down, from property in terms of land to any sort of property, then to taxpaying, then toward a goal of admitting all free white adult males as voters. The process of change was not even and in no two states were voting freedoms the same except by accident.

5

WHEN VERMONT was admitted to the Union in 1791 it was the only state with full white manhood suffrage. Its already established voting law, the most liberal in the country, required no property or taxpaying test. Any man could vote if he had lived there a year and was of "quiet and peaceable behavior."

In most states there was no sudden leap. Voting change came more slowly and not easily. But in almost every state there was a growing desire to vote by those still denied that right, and a new interest in the institutions of government in a country that at last had become free to manage its own affairs. The ordinary people, who had fought a war to govern themselves, found themselves in a new struggle, not of guns but of politics, in which votes became the weapons.

The formation of political parties was something the makers of the constitution had never expected to happen in the United States. They had planned for a perfect Union in which all factions hopefully would work together without political conflict and without dissent by the people.

But great numbers of the people did dissent from the Federalist view that instead of governing themselves they must be governed by a privileged class that Alexander Hamilton had described as "the rich, the well-born and the good." Believing as Thomas Jefferson did that the average run of mankind could govern themselves by their votes, they demanded the right to have those votes to support what was growing into the first genuinely American political party, the Jeffersonian Republicans.

Open debate, argument and freedom of political diversity alarmed the Founding Fathers, who feared that such divisions would tear the country apart. George Washington warned in his Farewell Address in 1796 that the growth of political party spirit would "distract the public councils and enfeeble the public administration," that it "agitates the community with ill-founded jealousies and false alarms; kindles the animosity of one part against another . . ."

John Adams, the next Federalist president, despised Thomas Jefferson's "democratical" thinking, warned against the democratic tendencies growing in the United States, and said, "There never was a democracy that did not commit suicide." The Federalist congress of his administration passed the Sedition Act that practically made it a crime for anybody to be a Republican. It provided jail sentences and heavy fines for those who dared criticize the president, congress or the federal government "with intent to defame or bring them . . . into contempt or disrepute."

But the people would not be silenced. With the power of their votes, they caused political revolution. The votes of small farmers, planters, frontiersmen and city workers helped sweep Jefferson and democracy into control in 1800 and also established the party system as a way of American political life, a system which in time became the enduring strength of popular government in the United States.

"The revolution of 1800," Jefferson himself said, "was as real a revolution in the principles of our government as that of 1776 was in its form; not effected indeed by the sword . . . but by the rational and peaceable instrument of reform, the suffrage of the people."

In the states, where the battles of voting reform had to be fought, not all Jeffersonians sided with those who wanted more liberal election laws and not all Federalists were opposed. Many men drew a line between what they thought was politically good for the nation and what they felt was needed in their own states. In Maryland, it was Michael Taney, a wealthy landowning Federalist, who first sponsored a bill calling for complete white manhood suffrage, and other Federalists carried on the fight for it.

Marylanders were able to get the legislation through the popularly elected House of Delegates several times, only to have it blocked by the state's senate where power was firmly in control of ultra-conservative men of property. They were well protected from the will of the people by a state constitution which said that those selected by the legislature to serve in the Senate not only had to be men of "wisdom, experience and virtue," but that they also had to own property worth at least one thousand pounds.

But the people found a way to force the Maryland senate to broaden their right to vote. The democratic majority in the House of Delegates threatened to call a convention to write a new constitution and change the rules for choosing senators. Rather than risk that the senators finally gave in and approved a bill that removed freehold and property restrictions. By 1810 every qualified male resident of Maryland who was free, white and twenty-one could vote.

South Carolina, the same year, lifted its taxpaying qualifications and extended the vote to all white males except soldiers and paupers. But the change there brought no real shift in political power since nobody could be elected to either house of the legislature unless he was a large property holder.

Connecticut was such a Federalist stronghold that its supreme court in 1802 sentenced a man for sedition just because he dared to advocate manhood suffrage. Politically the state still operated under the royal charter that had been given the colony in 1622 by Charles II, which entrenched men of property in public office where they proudly resisted all change "while the billows of democracy have beat upon us." But Jefferson's election in 1800 had shaken Connecticut too, and the fight for greater suffrage there was intense.

Republicans joined with other minority groups, elected a coalition and forced the calling of a constitutional convention that in 1818 finally broke the bonds of antiquated charter government. Connecticut didn't go all the way to full manhood suffrage, but the new constitution did give the vote to every male of "good moral character" who had served in the militia or who paid taxes.

Within some thirty years after the United States became a nation, property tests for voting were being washed away almost everywhere. Permitting taxpayers to vote was as far as some states would go for a while, but that was a gain over the old concept of property restrictions, and the tide was running strongly toward even more liberal voting rights.

Ohio and Louisiana entered the Union with taxpayer requirements and New Jersey and Massachusetts were among older states that soon rewrote their laws to include taxpayers as voters. Missouri, the first new state west of the Mississippi River, went further and gave the franchise to "every free white male citizen." The new state of Maine allowed all males to vote, "excepting paupers, persons under guardianship, and Indians not taxed." As other new states came in, Illinois and Alabama permitted all white males to vote, but Mississippi said they had to be taxpayers.

The new democracy was sweeping New York, where wealthy conservatives and lords of the manor had ruled over an almost feudal dynasty of political power and special privilege. Protected by a state constitution written in 1777 with strict property qualifications, their political stronghold had been in the enormous estates along the Hudson River, some of which had been held in family ownership since the early days of Dutch settlement.

Lording it over thousands of acres of land, their influence and economic power controlled enough votes to dominate government, until it was upset by the flooding of new settlers into the western part of the state and by the booming population growth in the city of New York. Finally, in 1821, a convention was called to write a new state constitution.

Delegates vowing to create a democratic state came to Albany determined to wipe out all property tests and give all men an equal right to vote. The new constitution gave the vote to taxpayers, to those who worked to improve roads around their farms, and to members of the militia. Five years later the taxpaying restrictions were removed from the constitution. An amendment gave the right to vote to every white male New Yorker who had lived in the state a year and in his own county six months.

In little Rhode Island there was a people's rebellion that threatened armed revolution in the struggle for more democratic voting freedom. Once mainly a farming state, Rhode Island was shifting to an industrial society with a growing population of city workers who were voteless because they owned no land. Landowner politicians, still clinging to the property protections of the old colonial charter granted by the King of England two hundred years before, arrogantly rejected even the most moderate appeals for suffrage reform.

They claimed the absolute right of those who owned the land to govern it, but there wasn't enough land in the whole state to qualify the majority of people as voters.

Finally a compromise produced a constitution that set up two kinds of voting privileges in Rhode Island. Qualified property owners could vote after living in the state only a year and all naturalized citizens had to be landowners before they could vote. But native white males who had lived in Rhode Island two years no longer needed to be landowners for voting. They could vote if they simply paid a one-dollar tax, which amounted to a registry fee, and they didn't have to pay even that if they had done military service.

By 1845 absolute property restrictions on voting without any alternative had been abolished in all but two states, Virginia and North Carolina. Virginia, where mighty battles for suffrage reform had gone on for half a century, finally gave in and eliminated both property and taxpaying qualifications in 1850, granting the vote to all white male citizens of the United States who had lived in Virginia two years. North Carolina's landowners held out for property tests until 1856, when the state finally admitted taxpayers as voters.

In most states even taxpaying qualifications soon were removed or reduced. Democracy, once a feared and hated concept, had become accepted, and Americans generally favored white manhood suffrage. But those who had won the right to vote usually had to be native-born free white males over the age of twenty-one, which still left out a lot of people. In addition, in various states there were specific restrictions which kept not only women, paupers and blacks from voting, but Indians, Chinese, Catholics, Jews or others, according to local and regional prejudices.

There was still a wide gap between the right to vote and a man's freedom at the polling places to cast his vote for candidates of his choice. From the beginning, Americans also had been fighting for that right to vote freely, without intimidation, and to have their votes counted honestly.

6

When American voters today step into a booth to cast their ballot they take it for granted that the choice is nobody's business but their own. But that was a right few earlier Americans had. For years no man's vote was really secret, or protected from influence, bribery, threats and dishonesty. It was only by hard battle and long reform that Americans made the secret ballot the main working tool of democratic government.

In most of colonial America elections were decided by voice vote or a show of hands, which was simpler than written ballots when the colonies were small. It also meant that every elected official knew exactly who his friends were and could hand out rewards or deny them accordingly. If a voter voiced a choice not approved by men of power and influence in a community he might risk his social standing or even his income. With his vote no secret from anybody he was almost certain to displease at least some of his neighbors who voted the other way.

Men armed with clubs or guns marched on some polling places to intimidate voters. Fist fights and brawls were even more frequent. Liquor supplied by rival candidates was consumed by the barrel and drunkenness was common. Each arriving voter walked a gauntlet of those who crowded around as he approached the table where a magistrate or sheriff sat to hear him publicly declare his vote. Sometimes the voting was done in an open field or outdoors in front of a courthouse. Cheers or boos might greet the voter's declaration, back-slapping approval or the threat of being beaten up afterwards.

As more men won the right to vote, the demand for written ballots grew, especially in heavily populated areas, and by the time of the Revolution voting by written papers was accepted in some colonies although not always required by law. In New York the ballot reform movement started as early as 1734, but gained no real support until after 1760 when the intimidation of voters became so violent there was great public scandal.

A bill for balloting was put before the New York legislature in 1769, but was denounced as a scheme to cloak politicians in secrecy. Defenders of the voice vote called for preserving that method by which "every Elector is at Liberty to declare the Sentiments of his Heart," and by a narrow margin the voice vote was kept. In 1777 New York authorized paper ballots for the election of governor, but not till ten years later was balloting allowed for members of the legislature. By that time the lawmakers admitted that "an opinion has long prevailed among divers of the Good People of this State that voting at elections by ballot would tend more to preserve the liberty and equal freedom of the people."

Virginia firmly rejected all suggestions for balloting and kept its colonial method of voice voting when it became a state. Some elections by voice were still being held in Virginia up to the time of the Civil War. Kentucky flirted briefly with the idea of using paper ballots by adopting a law that provided for them in 1792, but seven years later went back to voice voting and became the last of all the states to abandon it entirely in 1891.

But Vermont in 1793, Tennessee three years later, and then other states, favored the written ballot. The new democracy and the rise of political parties, as well as the gradual lifting of property restrictions, shifted the thrust of American suffrage reform from the bare right to vote to the manner in which the voting was done. In the Northwest Territory the abuses of voice voting brought a change to paper balloting in 1800 and it wasn't long after that before most states were using ballots.

However the first so-called "secret ballots" soon turned out to be anything but secret. Politicians made balloting a tool to enforce party influence and many voters discovered they had no more privacy of choice than in voice voting. Some politically inspired laws required the voter to sign his name to the ballot which let everybody know how he had voted, or else made him show his open ballot to poll officials before dropping it into the box.

There was no such thing as an official ballot issued to all voters alike. Each voter had to write his own ballot by hand and almost any scrap of paper might be used. As party politics grew so did the lists of possible candidates for a great number of offices and writing out a ballot by hand became a laborious task.

Some people sought help from politicians who offered to write their ballots for them. All a voter had to do was choose a ballot written by a party he favored and carry the prepared slip to the polling place to drop into the box, which was fine for the politician but left the voter with no freedom to choose anyone the party had not endorsed.

As the practice gradually became more widespread parties began to issue printed ballots. Massachusetts tried to reject them but the state's supreme court decided in 1829 that printed votes were written votes within the meaning of the law and in other states there were court rulings to the same effect. Maine in 1831, and Vermont and Connecticut shortly afterwards, passed laws to authorize either printed or handwritten ballots and in most states the idea that a voter should write his own ballot soon gave way to the use of printed ballots distributed by political parties.

Each party leader printed his own ballots, some of which looked like railroad tickets so that people began to call them "party tickets." The ballot became still less secret when politicians took to printing their tickets on colored paper. Each party chose a distinctive color so poll watchers could tell at a glance which ticket a man voted. That led to such bribery and intimidation that nearly all the states tried in some way to put a stop to it.

Maine outlawed colored ballots and required political parties to print them on clean white paper, but the politicians quickly discovered there were many shades of white and different textures of paper and that ballots also could be cut or folded in tell-tale ways. Massachusetts in 1851 and Rhode Island at about the same time started providing envelopes for city and town officials to distribute on election day so voters could conceal their ballots in them. Several states issued official paper upon which party ballots could be printed so they would all look alike outwardly. But the politicians still did the printing and distributing and usually found a way to get around whatever protective devices the states adopted.

Candidates for office each had to pay the party a large fee for printing and distributing ballots, which often became a cover-up to raise party funds to buy votes and otherwise corrupt the elections. Such funds frequently were used to recruit drifters who were led from one polling place to another to repeat their votes.

Stuffing ballot boxes also was easy when ballots were printed on all different sorts of paper. A common method was for a party voter to hide half a dozen folded tissue paper ballots inside his own ballot so that when he dropped his into the box the others went in with it. The lack of official ballots encouraged many forms of cheating as well as much juggling in the listing of candidates since the states had little control over deliberate "errors" in printing. Crooked politicians sometimes made a deal to leave a candidate's name off the ballot entirely so the opposing candidate, for the price of a fat bribe, would be sure to win.

There were many reform attempts but Americans generally voted with party ballots until nearly the beginning of the 20th Century. The real reform in balloting in the United States started in Australia. Elections there had been as corrupt as they were almost everywhere else until Victoria in 1857 pioneered with a law requiring the use of an official ballot that was printed and distributed by the government, with elaborate provisions to end party influence and protect secret voting. Southern Australia, Tasmania

and New South Wales adopted similar secret ballot laws
the following year, with results that were so dramatic in
ending election disorders and cheating that the fame of the
Australian Ballot soon spread throughout the world.

The success of the new ballot in Australia brought tests
of it in various cities in England that soon produced more
orderly elections. After investigations by committees of
Parliament, the British House of Commons in 1872 passed
a law to replace oral voting in Britain with the Australian
secret ballot. Belgium, Luxembourg, Italy and other countries began adopting it and the Australian Ballot became a
major reform issue of the 1880's and 1890's in the United
States.

It was an era when many groups were crusading for government tax, land and labor reforms and the leaders of
such other causes took up the Australian Ballot as a means
of giving the people greater voting power to overcome the
control of the political bosses who often stood in the way
of social change. Pamphlets, speeches, newspaper editorials
and attempts to put bills for the Australian Ballot before
state legislatures gave it nationwide publicity.

Henry George, the economist who founded the single tax
movement with its theory that the land belonged to the
people and that those who monopolized the use of it should
pay the entire cost of government, was among the most influential pioneers of the Australian Ballot in the United
States.

As a boy of fourteen he had worked his way to Australia
aboard a sailing ship and had returned to California to become a typesetter, newspaper editor and writer. While

working out his land and tax theories, he had become convinced that Australia could show America the way in balloting.

George was among the first to advocate the Australian Ballot in print in an article he wrote for the *Overland Monthly* in 1871. He soon became far more famous as the author of *Progress and Poverty* which was read by millions and gained an enormous popular following for his single tax movement. After he moved to New York as a writer and lecturer, he used his new influence in a continuing fight for the Australian Ballot. He came close to being elected mayor of New York, edited a single tax newspaper read throughout the country which contained appeals for the Australian Ballot, organized a Ballot Reform League, and helped to form a United Labor Party which was the first national political party to demand the new ballot in its platform, before the reform had swept the rest of the country.

"Since the ballot is the only means by which in our republic the redress of political and social grievances is to be sought," the party platform declared, the "Australian system of voting" was needed to "prevent bribery and intimidation, do away with practical discriminations in favor of the rich and unscrupulous, and lessen the pernicious influence of money in politics."

In his own writings George called the Australian Ballot "the one primary reform that will make easier all the other reforms." He won support for the ballot from labor leaders, farm groups and others, and personally encouraged those who were beginning legislative battles for it in the states. An article he wrote for the *North American Review* in March, 1883, in which he urged the Australian Ballot as "the greatest single reform," helped bring about the first such law adopted anywhere in the United States.

Among the readers it influenced was Arthur Wallace, a member of the Kentucky legislature. With the support of a group interested in ballot reform Wallace drafted a law to amend the city charter of Louisville, which was passed in February, 1888. The nation's first Australian Ballot law, modeled on the law in use in England, applied only to elections in Louisville. But it was such an immediate success in checking election abuses there that it was extended the following year to other heavily populated cities and counties and gradually to much of the state. Kentucky, which by paradox would be the last of all the states to abandon oral voting entirely, thus became the first where the Australian Ballot was put to direct test in municipal elections.

Massachusetts, later the same year of 1888, was first to adopt a statewide Australian Ballot law, due mainly to the efforts of Richard Henry Dana III, one of Boston's social and intellectual elite, an attorney, noted sportsman, son-in-law of Henry Wadsworth Longfellow, and member of a family that for generations had distinguished itself in law, literature and politics.

Dana's concern was because of his belief that the rough-and-tumble of corrupt politics kept many other wealthy and socially prominent men from seeking office and providing what he thought should be their example and leadership in good government. He drew up a proposed ballot bill and used his considerable influence to have it introduced in the legislature, argued for it before legislative committees, and helped push it through to a vote.

In May, 1888, the Massachusetts legislature passed it.

Under the new law party ballots were replaced by official state ballots that were to be printed at public expense. They were to be distributed only by election officers at the polling places and were to contain the names of all candidates nominated by party convention or direct petition of the voters. The law included detailed provisions, also drawn up by Dana, for voting booths and other innovations to secure secrecy in the casting of ballots. He had carpenters build sample booths to his specifications so voters, who were accustomed to simply dropping prepared party ballots into the slot, could be instructed in the new method of voting.

The first test of the Massachusetts law was in the elections of November, 1889, and it proved such a success that the law became a model for reformers in other states. Voting was fair and orderly, more voters turned out than usual, and the added cost to the state was small. Newspapers and national magazines praised the new way of voting and the proof in Massachusetts that it would work greatly strengthened the movement elsewhere.

Debates over the secret ballot already were underway in many states. By 1890 thirteen states and territories had adopted some form of the Australian Ballot. The number grew to twenty by the end of the century and by 1910 voters in nearly all the United States, with a few exceptions, had won the right to a secret ballot, issued, supervised and protected by state government.

They had taken the printing and distribution of ballots out of the hands of the political parties, and if they hadn't swept away all the corruption of the polling places they had ended some of the worst of it. But what Americans called the Australian Ballot was not the ballot the Australians had introduced. That was short, simple and non-partisan, which the American version never was. Because of the established American party system most states provided for party voting, and because of the great number of candidates running for various offices the American ballots became long and complex.

Some states listed candidates according to political parties in what amounted to transferring all the old separate party tickets to one sheet of paper, listed side by side. Other states divided their ballot listings according to offices being sought, with all the candidates for each office grouped together and each name identified by a party symbol. About half the states issued general election ballots that included all levels of government and all issues that were to be put before the voters on one large sheet.

The long and complicated paper ballots made the hand-counting of votes a slow process, subject to manipulation by dishonest election officials and to the honest errors of weary vote counters. Faulty counts, deliberate or otherwise, were frequent and recounts difficult. For years before the Australian Ballot the use of machines had been suggested to speed the voting process and eliminate some of the fraud and error.

Vote reformers in England had proposed what was probably the first one in 1836, a ballot box fitted with cards the voter could punch by sticking a pointed rod through the holes of a wooden frame. There were many other early devices invented, including one patented by Thomas Edison in 1869, but none of them was actually ever tested in elections. It wasn't until the late 1800's when states first began to adopt the Australian Ballot that they had any urgent need for voting machines.

Almost overnight dozens of makes and models appeared. New York enacted the first voting machine law in 1892, authorizing their use for the election of town officers in any town that approved of them. Like laws first passed in other states, it made the use of machines optional. Rhode Island in 1900 bought and furnished some to cities and towns that asked for them.

Courts in some states decided a mechanical vote was as legal as a written vote, but in others the state election laws had to be amended to permit mechanical voting. Many of the first machines were subject to breakdowns and so easy to tamper with that after unhappy experiences several states repealed their new laws and returned to paper ballots. Approval of them was more enthusiastic as the machines were improved.

Full use of voting machines came slowly. Twenty-one states had authorized their optional use by 1911 but by 1934 only nine states and parts of six others were using them. Even in 1952 it was estimated that only forty-two percent of all votes cast in the presidential election of that year were by machine. After that the trend toward voting by machines was more rapid.

The machine itself had become the voting booth, curtaining each voter with individual privacy at the touch of a lever, presenting him with an official and approved form of ballot, mechanically and secretly registering the free choices he made according to his conscience. It was no guarantee in itself of honest elections, but if there were still grave faults in the election system the gravest of them were no longer in the method of casting the ballot.

7

THE AMERICAN PEOPLE were guaranteed no constitutional right to vote for the president and vice-president of the United States. It was a right they took for themselves. The constitution did not require any popular vote or popular national election and did not say who was entitled to vote for president or whether anybody could vote at all. But the people gradually hammered out their own system of presidential elections.

Working within the framework of the constitution, they changed the intent of those who wrote it and assumed for themselves the power to choose the president. They still have not won the right to vote for presidential candidates directly, or to hold one national presidential election instead of fifty separate elections in the various states, but they have nearly brought about the change to a direct vote for the president by all the people.

The Founding Fathers who gathered in Philadelphia in 1787 had more trouble deciding how the president should be chosen than they had in writing any other part of the constitution. They had to satisfy the interests of small states that were afraid of being overwhelmed by big states, had to find some device that would reflect the will of the people and at the same time preserve the sovereign rights of the states, and had to produce a political solution that would win ratification of the constitution by the states.

They came very close to letting congress choose the president. Delegates voted for such a plan four different times and favored it until the last debates. The main objection to it was that the president might become a "mere creature" of congress, without executive independence.

There were some delegates who urged that the people be allowed to vote directly for president. Pennsylvania's Gouverneur Morris argued for direct election on the grounds that the nation's chief executive should be "the guardian of the people, even of the lower classes." Virginia's James Madison agreed that direct election was the plan he liked best, even "with all its imperfections."

But not many delegates were willing to entrust the choice of president directly to the people. The feeling was that most Americans of that time knew little about affairs beyond the borders of their own states and that the presidential decision should be made for them to avoid the quarrels and disorders of popular voting.

"The people are uninformed and would be misled by a few designing men," Elbridge Gerry of Massachusetts warned. Virginia's George Mason held that "it would be as unnatural to refer the choice of a proper magistrate to the people as it would to refer the trial of colors to a blind man." Roger Sherman of Connecticut believed that if the people could vote for president they would "generally vote for some man in their own state."

Twice the Constitutional Convention overwhelmingly

turned down proposals to allow the choice of president by
direct election. Finally, seeking a compromise hardly any
of them had favored in the beginning, they developed the
system of intermediate electors that was written into the
constitution.

The legislature of each state, elected by the people, was
to "appoint" a certain number of presidential electors.
Throughout the country, the electors would meet in each of
their states on the same specified day, and each elector
would ballot secretly for two persons at least one of whom
did not live in that state. The results would be sent to congress for counting.

Whoever had a majority of the electoral votes would be
president, and after that the next highest would be vice-
president. If there was no majority for president then the
election would be thrown into the House of Representatives for decision. A constitutional amendment later
changed part of the original plan so that the electors cast
separate ballots for president and vice-president, but the
basic electoral system remained.

The framers of the constitution had completely avoided
the question of suffrage in the choice of the nation's chief
executive. The number of presidential electors each state
was entitled to have was not related to the number of its
voters. Whether a state was large or small it would have
two electors, just as it had two senators, plus as many more
electors as it had representatives in congress, which meant
electoral votes were to be based on a state's total population, including women, children and other non-voters as
well as voters.

Each state was left entirely free to choose presidential

electors without any specific qualifications and in any way
it pleased. The electors from each state were to be appointed, the constitution said, "in such manner as the legislature thereof may direct." They could be chosen by the
members of the legislature itself, by anybody else the legislature wanted to designate, or they could be chosen by the
voters of a state if the legislature wished to allow a popular
election. But no state was obliged by the constitution to
let its people vote for presidential electors.

It was the hope of at least some of the Founding Fathers
that the system of intermediate electors would safeguard
the choice of president from the factional disputes that
might be caused by direct elections. Ideally the chosen
electors would be prominent citizens of each state, men
well-informed about national affairs, who would indepen-
dently search the whole country to propose for election the
men best-suited to lead it.

But what the constitution actually gave the state legislatures amounted to an open invitation to manipulate the
electoral process in any way that suited their immediate
political desires. The voters, in the beginning, had very
little to say about the choice of the president. In the first
presidential elections of 1789 there was no close contest
since nearly everybody favored George Washington, but
in almost every state there were disputes over the method
of choosing presidential electors.

Five of the legislatures of states then in the Union simply
appointed their electors, without giving the people any
voice at all. They were Connecticut, Delaware, Georgia,
New Jersey and South Carolina. The New York legislature
decided to do the same thing, but the members of its two

houses argued so long over the choice that they were still in deadlock on the day electors were to vote and New York lost its first presidential votes entirely.

Massachusetts allowed duly qualified voters to nominate presidential electors by districts, but left their final election up to the legislature, which also chose two of the electors itself without any prior nomination by the voters. New Hampshire planned to leave the choice of electors to the people, but its system was so complicated that none of the electors received a popular majority so the New Hampshire legislature also wound up choosing the electors itself. In the end, Pennsylvania, Maryland and Virginia were the only three states in which voters actually elected the men who would "elect" George Washington as president.

By the time of the second presidential elections in 1792, the ruling Federalists faced the rising opposition of the new Republicans, whose forces soon were to center around Thomas Jefferson, and many of the legislatures took full advantage of their power to appoint electors who would sway votes to one side or the other. The legislatures of nine of the fifteen states chose the electors themselves, two more legislatures chose some of the electors, and only four states left the choice entirely to the voters.

Four years later, in the 1796 elections, most of the state legislatures again appointed the presidential electors themselves. But by then any pretense that presidential elections were non-political was being swept away. The contest for the presidency became an open party battle, with both parties nominating candidates by a poll of their members in congress, and the role of the electors was forever changed.

The presidential electors were no longer a group of supposedly disinterested men with some freedom of choice, but were men who were expected to cast their votes for the candidates already nominated by the parties. As the party system grew, the constitutional ideal of the electors vanished, so that they became puppets of the political parties, themselves chosen by each party, hardly more than a device for counting the vote.

In the close and bitter election of 1800, which finally was decided in the House of Representatives where it took thirty-six ballots to break the deadlock and make Jefferson president, leading politicians of both parties rigged the methods of choosing presidential electors in key states. In ten of the sixteen states the legislatures picked electors and gave the people no vote.

The crisis of 1800 made many Americans aware of the fact that the will of the people might be frustrated in any close election, just as the open political battling had made a myth of the idea that electors had any real say in choosing the president. As the new democracy grew, so did the belief that the chief executive should be truly the people's president, and the people increasingly demanded the right to elect the electors.

But their battle for the right to vote for presidential electors had to be fought out state by state. For another quarter of a century ruling politicians in each state continued to shift the methods of choosing electors. With the constitutional freedom to do as they pleased, the legislatures slanted the election laws to favor whatever party was in command, so the people hardly knew from one election to the next whether they would be allowed to vote for president.

"The discordant systems adopted by the different states," Senator Mahlon Dickerson of New Jersey complained in 1818, "are the subject of constant fluctuation and change— of frequent, hasty and ra'sh experiment—established, altered, abolished, re-established, according to the dictates of the interest, ambition, the whim or caprice of party and fashion."

Until the 1820's many state legislatures went on appointing electors, a method politicians favored because it avoided the unpredictable results of a direct vote by the people. Where people had been granted a vote, politicians in power often took it from them whenever there seemed to be a chance that the popular vote might go to the other party.

But public outrage grew, along with the demand for popular voting, and legislators who denied the people a presidential vote frequently found themselves voted out of office at the next election. As the legislatures were forced to answer to the people, they gradually abandoned the appointment of electors.

The battle between the people and the legislatures was fought out, over and over, in state elections and in conventions to draft new state constitutions. Basically it was a battle to change the old concept that individual citizens should not choose the president. It reached its climax in 1828 when the "Democracy of Numbers" swept Andrew Jackson into the White House.

Four years before, in 1824, only about 356,000 Americans had voted for president, but by 1828 the number of voters swelled to more than 1,155,000. The people by then had won the right to vote for presidential electors in all but two of the states. Delaware and South Carolina were the only two where the legislatures still appointed them, and Delaware yielded to the people in 1832. South Carolina alone finally held out against the trend toward democracy until the Civil War.

Democratic ideals had advanced so far by the 1820's that the people of most states were unwilling to leave the crucial choice of presidential electors in the hands of the legislatures. They also began to force upon the states what gradually developed into a national method of presidential elections by the general ticket system, under which all electors ran for election on a statewide basis. It was the simplest and most direct system, providing for the popular choice of electors according to their party loyalties.

Some states had allowed voters to choose electors by geographical districts, a plan considered the fairest of all by many of the nation's most distinguished early statesmen, including Jefferson, Hamilton, Madison, Jackson and John Quincy Adams. In theory, people who voted by districts might choose some electors of one party and some of another, and opposition votes would not be wiped out as they were when a statewide election gave all the state's electors to the majority party.

But there was no uniformity in creating the districts, which were often manipulated by the legislatures along with the voting rights allowed within them. After 1820 the district system gave way to statewide elections, which a few of the states had used from the beginning. The statewide general ticket system suited not only the majority of the people but also the ruling politicians.

With a statewide election by general ticket the majority party in each state could deliver a solid block of electoral votes to its national candidates. Eighteen of the states were choosing presidential electors by the general ticket system of statewide voting in 1828, forcing many other states to follow so their strength in the electoral college would not be diluted. By 1836 the general ticket system had been adopted by every state in the Union except South Carolina.

As the states began enacting somewhat parallel laws, presidential elections fell into a general pattern. In each state political parties nominated their own lists of electors who promised to cast their electoral votes for that party's candidates for president and vice-president. Voters elected the electors according to the parties they represented and the party that got most of the state's popular votes got all of that state's electoral votes.

The presidential electors became almost forgotten men whose names were seldom known to the average voter who elected them. In recent years the shortened forms of ballots used in many states have not even bothered to list individual electors by name. Most Americans hardly realize that they are voting for electors instead of for presidential candidates or that the real decision as to who will become president is not made on election day every fourth November but two months later, after the electors have voted and their votes have been counted.

Through the years the people's right to vote in presidential elections has become so accepted that it is often spoken of as a constitutional right. But the constitution merely permitted the states to grant that privilege if they so desired. People vote for presidential electors only because each individual state has voluntarily allowed them to choose electors that way. Under the constitution, any state legislature theoretically could adopt some other method and deny its people the right to vote for president at any time.

South Carolina's legislature continued to appoint that state's presidential electors until 1860. The newly reconstructed state of Florida did so in 1868 and so did the newly admitted state of Colorado in 1876. In Michigan in 1892 politicians in control of the state legislature tried to divide the state's electoral votes by switching from statewide elections to the district system. Federal courts in each case upheld the basic constitutional right of the states to "appoint" electors as they pleased.

At least in theory, a state legislature can refuse to take part in a presidential election at all or it can vest the power to choose presidential electors in the board of directors of a bank, a highway commission, or in any group of men who happen along the street. But, with rare exceptions, people have been permitted by the states to elect the electors on a statewide basis since 1836 and it is highly unlikely that any state legislature today would attempt to take from the people the presidential voting rights they have won.

8

WHEN THE FOUNDING FATHERS created congress they deliberately protected the Senate, as they had the presidency, from the direct influence of America's voters. As a conservative upper house the Senate was meant to serve as the collective voice of the states to balance the lower branch of congress where the people had their voice through elected representatives. Written into the constitution was the provision: "The Senate of the United States shall be composed of two Senators from each State, chosen by the Legislature thereof . . ."

For one hundred and twenty-four years senators were elected by the legislatures of the states, not by the people, and the Senate became an aristocratic chamber unique among democratic institutions, an American House of Lords whose members established their own nobility. But after more than a century in which no senator had to answer directly to the public will, the power of the people changed the whole concept of the Senate as a branch of government over which they had been given no control.

The people again created their own right to vote. Denied that right, they finally took the power of choosing senators

into their own hands, and at last forced the Senate itself
to yield on an amendment to the constitution that gave
them the right to elect senators.

It was a demand that was slow in growing and it came
as much from the chaotic troubles caused in the states by
the legislative election of senators as from public desire to
end the domination of the Senate by political bosses and
men of great wealth.

The states vied with each other in the beginning to
send the Senate their most eloquent and distinguished men,
who made it a vital forum and the center of the nation's
statesmanship. It wasn't until around the mid-1800's that
the people generally began to complain about the quality
of the senators elected by their legislatures. But they had
complained long before that over the method of election
that turned the legislatures of many states into raging political battlegrounds.

The capture of a senate seat, with its federal patronage
in jobs and funds and its enormous influence, became the
first prize of warring politicians in the states, often the key
to the entrenched power of boss-controlled political machines that dominated the states.

Furious party battles over the legislative election of senators caused such confusion, corruption and crippling delay
that all the activities of state government suffered. Legislation the people wanted and needed was blocked while
legislatures fought over what frequently was the choice of
a senator not because he would best serve the state and nation but because he would best serve the party and its boss.

With the relatively small number of votes of members
of the legislature to be won, bought or bargained for by

politicians and lobbyists for special interests, intense campaigning for the Senate began months before a legislature
met. Days before the legislative session began, state lawmakers arriving in the capital city would be wined and
dined in the hotel rooms various politicians set up as head-
quarters. Although there was no popular vote involved,
the electioneering for the votes of the legislature went on
day and night.

The real choice was often made by party caucus in
smoke-filled rooms behind the scenes. In states where one
party held tight machine control some bosses had themselves elected to the Senate. Others made sure of the re-
election of a senator who had served them well in Washington in previous terms. But in states where factions were
battling for power the political war often went on for weeks
or months while other legislative activities were delayed.

Election in most states meant that a candidate for the
Senate had to win a majority of the votes in both houses.
If one party controlled one branch of the legislature and
another party the other branch the balloting could go on
day after day, with both sides desperately struggling to
break the deadlock. Sometimes there was no break and the
session ended with the state unable to elect anybody to the
Senate. That left it with only one senator in Washington,
deprived of equal representation, and it also deprived the
Senate of its full membership.

Such deadlocks didn't happen frequently or in all the
states, but by the end of the Civil War, deadlocks and challenges had become so frequent that public demand forced
the Senate to exercise the long-neglected constitutional
power of congress to regulate the elections.

The Senate Judiciary Committee drew up a law intended to provide a uniform method of electing senators by the state legislatures, but there were sharp differences of opinion in the Senate over every detail and by the time it finally came to a vote the proposed law was filled with so many loopholes and confusions critics charged that it encouraged many of the evils it was meant to eliminate. Thirteen members of the Senate absented themselves from the voting when it was passed and sent to the House of Representatives, where it was adopted without debate in a rush to prevent further efforts to block it.

The new law went into effect July 25, 1866, and despite its soon obvious defects the Senate rejected all attempts to change it for the next forty-seven years. It required state legislatures to elect senators by an extremely complicated procedure that was open at almost every step to political pressures.

First the two houses of the legislature were to meet separately and each was to name a senator by voice vote. On the following day both houses were to meet jointly and present the results of their separate votes. If it turned out that each house had given a majority to the same candidate then he would be the state's elected senator. But if he had failed to win the separate majority vote of each house then the two branches of the legislature must meet in joint assembly at noon of each succeeding day for as long as the legislature was in session and vote at least once each day until a senator had been elected.

During the years the law was in effect, nearly half the states in the Union suffered serious legislative deadlocks at one time or another. Charges of bribery were frequent and in some legislatures there were fist-fights, near riots and threats of armed assault. In senatorial elections from 1891 to 1905 there were forty-five deadlocks, from one to seven in each of twenty states scattered from Delaware to California. Some went on for more than one hundred days while legislatures voted as many as two hundred times, often without finally electing any senator at all.

Legislatures became frantic as a deadlocked session neared adjournment. With so much at stake, politicians brought the darkest of dark horses into the race at the last minute, hoping to elect almost anybody to snatch victory for the party. On a single day a legislature might ballot as many as fifty times for an assortment of up to eighty candidates in the wild hope that one of them could win election. Stampeded elections were common as the final hours of a session turned legislatures into brawls with men climbing on desks and chairs, waving their arms and shouting threats at each other.

In Utah in 1897 the Republicans tried to stop the clock on the wall of the assembly chamber to prevent adjournment, but when they dragged up a ladder the Democrats seized it and hurled it through a window. Fist-fights broke out, desks were torn from the floor, books and inkwells were thrown. Republicans smashed the glass of the clock and finally broke the pendulum to keep it from ticking away the minutes.

There was nearly armed warfare in Colorado in 1903 when the two houses of the legislature, each controlled by a different party, tried to unseat enough opposing legislators on charges of fraud to swing a senatorial election. One party was backed by the Denver police force and the other appealed to the governor for state troops to fight the police, but calmer heads finally prevailed and open warfare was averted.

In Kentucky a few years earlier the govenror had to call out the militia to keep pistol-carrying members of the legislature from making good their threats to settle the election of a senator by shooting at each other. For three days the legislature met under the guard of troops enforcing martial law.

Fourteen seats were left vacant in the Senate by deadlocked legislatures between 1891 and 1905. Some states, at extra cost to their taxpayers, called legislatures back into special session to try again to agree on a senator and some of the special sessions were also deadlocked. Governors of five states tried to solve the dilemma by appointing senators to fill vacancies, but the Senate refused to seat the appointed men.

The public disgust over deadlocks, senate vacancies, neglect of ordinary state business and endless political warfare brought a public desire to do away with the legislative election of senators. Many Americans saw no good reason why they shouldn't choose their own senators just as they chose members of the House of Representatives. They began to support demands, not for better regulation by congress of senatorial elections, but for a change in the constitution itself to make senators directly answerable to the voters.

Back in 1826 the first resolution for a constitutional amendment to allow the popular election of senators was put before congress by Representative Henry Storrs of New York, but it was tabled without debate, and ten years later a similar resolution met the same fate. During the years between 1850 and 1855 five such resolutions were introduced, but hardly anybody took them seriously and they never got out of committee.

Andrew Johnson, then a young congressman from Tennessee, sponsored two of the resolutions. His experience as a member of his state legislature had convinced him the change was needed and he fought for it stubbornly through his whole political life. As a senator in 1860, Johnson renewed his crusade, and after he became president he sent congress two messages in 1868 to urge a constitutional amendment for direct senatorial elections. But his efforts had little effect on a congress which had sought to impeach him because of the bitterness that boiled out of Reconstruction after the Civil War.

The real demand came from the people who in the 1870's began bombarding congress with pleas and petitions from all parts of the country. In 1874 the legislatures of California and Iowa set an example soon followed by other legislatures and appealed to congress in the name of their states for action to provide for the election of senators by the people.

Individual congressmen, urged by voters in their states, introduced dozens of resolutions calling for constitutional amendment, all of which were pigeon-holed in committee where petitions and memorials to congress also were allowed to die. Before the change finally came in 1912 a total of 287 congressional resolutions had been introduced.

It wasn't until 1892 that the House Committee on Elections favorably reported out a resolution for the submission of the proposed amendment to the states. Five times in the next ten years, it was brought to a vote in the House, and each time it was overwhelmingly approved.

But there was no such approval in the Senate whose members didn't have to answer to any pressure from the voters. The Senate was not about to yield its constitutional security or risk the possibility that senators safely sent to Washington by their legislatures might be thrown out of office next election time by popular vote.

There were a few ardent advocates of change in the Senate but their resolutions, along with all public petitions, were referred to committees which for years simply ignored them. Not once in all the years until 1911 was the proposed amendment allowed to come to a senate vote. Without senate approval no constitutional amendment was possible. All the clamor in the House was futile because the Senate would not approve.

If the Senate had always been a house of special privilege, it was never more so than in the years of booming industrial and corporate growth that followed the Civil War. By the late 1800's the Senate was dominated by senators of great wealth and those who represented the wealthy. Big business and the politicians had formed an alliance that flourished in an America rapidly changing from an agricultural nation to a land of spreading cities, railroads, factories, commerce and giant monopolies of trade and finance.

Called a millionaire's club, the Senate was a fortress of protection for the special interests it served. There were railroad senators, oil senators, lumber, coal, sugar trust, and iron and steel senators, utility, commodity, and silver, gold and copper senators. They fought against government controls and regulation, against labor, safety, conservation and business tax measures, and generally obstructed all liberal legislation that might benefit the people at the cost of profit to the corporate and industrial groups they represented.

Supporting high tariffs and other laws that favored the trusts and monopolies, the senators boosted the prices of almost everything ordinary Americans needed to buy. Accused of an arrogant public-be-damned attitude that ignored the social needs of the nation's changing economy, they earned the growing outrage of reformers, writers and cartoonists who pictured them as a "Senate of Shame."

The people's demand for popular control of the Senate became insistent. The call for a constitutional amendment was voiced by candidates in state elections. National political parties took it up. The Populists endorsed a constitutional amendment in 1892. Democrats first made it a plank in their party's platform in 1900. Republicans rejected it, but the rising young Republican Progressives became new crusaders for it, battling the Old Guard within their own party.

Farm asociations, granges, labor organizations and civic groups joined in the petitioning. By the early 1900's more than two-thirds of all the states officially had asked for action by congress. In several states the question had been put to a direct test vote by referendum and was overwhelmingly approved by voters.

But against all pressure and despite the fact that the House of Representatives had voted five times for the proposed amendment, the Senate still refused to consider it. Faced with the seemingly impassable barrier of senate opposition, all congressional action halted for a time.

Tired of waiting, the people of some states took the election of senators into their own hands. They created their own right to vote by methods which side-stepped the constitution. Oregon led the way by enacting a law under which voters could express their choice for the Senate in a general election, with candidates for seats in the state legislature pledged at the same time to accept the result of the popular senatorial vote. Whoever was chosen senator by the voters was formally elected by the new legislature.

It worked so well that other states followed Oregon's lead with variations until finally twenty-nine states had framed methods by which their voters could indirectly elect senators. Many Progressive Republicans, liberal Democrats and others determined to reform the Senate and end its obstruction were among the new senators sent to Washington. Themselves chosen by the people, they became strong advocates within the Senate for the constitutional amendment that the old senate conservatives had always blocked.

Meanwhile the people, through their state legislatures, also gave new force and direction to the petitions for constitutional change. Pennsylvania's legislature appointed a committee to confer with the legislatures of other states. The result was a conference report that declared since the Senate had persistently refused to join in proposing the amendment for direct election of senators, the only hope of the states was to use a never-tried provision of the constitution and issue a call for a whole new Constitutional Convention of the United States.

Under the constitution, if two-thirds of the states made such a demand congress would be forced to call a Constitutional Convention, the first since the constitution was written by the Founding Fathers. Instead of sending congress petitions "most respectfully requesting" action on the amendment, which the Senate had ignored for years, the legislatures began bluntly petitioning congress "to forthwith call a Constitutional Convention."

The mere possibility of that severely shook senate conservatives. Once assembled there would be no limit to the changes a Constitutional Convention might make. It might consider all sorts of radical changes in the Senate and the whole framework of government. Rather than risk such a threat some senators who had been totally opposed to the amendment for their popular election shifted their views in the face of what they saw as a far greater danger.

Gradually all the gathering forces began to turn the tide in the Senate. Faced with the insurgent newcomers who had been sent to the Senate by the choice of the people and with the threat of the states to call a Constitutional Convention, the Old Guard of the Senate no longer could refuse to consider the amendment. But they fought a bitter last-ditch struggle to kill or to cripple it.

Senator William Borah, a young Republican Progressive elected by the Idaho legislature under direct instruction from the voters, led the drive to push the amendment through the Senate. Early in 1911 he brought a resolution strongly favoring its adoption out of committee and into debate on the Senate floor. Backed by other insurgents Borah guided it through six weeks of argument, parliamentary maneuvering, delays and attempted changes, with conservatives fighting it all the way.

On February 28, 1911, just before the session of congress ended, the Senate for the first time in its history was brought to vote on the direct issue of the election of senators by the people. The resolution for the amendment failed to win a necessary two-thirds majority, but by a narrow five-vote margin that clearly indicated future victory.

Five weeks later a new congress convened in special session, bringing into office with it more new young senators chosen by people of their states, and both houses almost immediately introduced resolutions for the amendment.

The House of Representatives quickly and overwhelmingly approved, and in the Senate Borah once again led the resolution through a maze of opposition delays, until the Senate also yielded. But it took still another session before the Senate gave up a final struggle in conference committee and the proposed Seventeenth Amendment to the constitution cleared both houses in May, 1912.

Ratification by the states was swift. Within less than a year the legislatures of three-fourths of the states had approved. On May 31, 1913, President Woodrow Wilson's Secretary of State, William Jennings Bryan, proclaimed that the people had won the right to vote for their senators. They had taken the power of election away from the legislatures and had rewritten the constitution so that it declared: "The Senate of the United States shall be composed of two Senators from each state, elected by the *people* thereof."

9

Five women in the village of Seneca Falls, New York, decided to call a public meeting in July, 1848, and thus started the fight for woman's right to vote that would go on for three-quarters of a century. They arranged to hold the meeting in the village chapel, lined up a few speakers, and put a notice in the local paper that rather grandly called it a convention "to discuss the social and civil rights of woman."

It was mainly Elizabeth Stanton's idea. As the wife of abolitionist Henry Stanton she had been active in the crusade against Negro slavery, a movement which first gave many women the courage to speak out on public issues in an age when it was considered scandalous for any woman to address a public gathering. Those who did were denounced by press and clergy, taunted by men, and sometimes attacked by angry mobs. A man's wife and daughters legally were his chattels and women had few rights of any kind. Most women accepted the long-established tradition that the decisions of government, like those of the family, were made by males to be obeyed by females.

Elizabeth Stanton decided to use the Declaration of Independence as a model for the Seneca Falls convention's Declaration of Sentiments, substituting words that declared woman's independence from man in the same stirring language of rebellion. It was the first American document to spell out woman's grievances and the parlor table upon which it was written later became a historic exhibit at the Smithsonian Institution in Washington.

Holding that "all men and women are created equal" and that "the history of mankind is a history of repeated injuries and usurpations on the part of man toward woman," it declared that "in view of this entire disfranchisement of one-half the people in this country . . . and because women do feel themselves aggrieved, oppressed and fraudulently deprived of their most sacred rights, we insist that they have immediate admission to all rights and privileges which belong to them as Citizens of the United States."

Nearly one hundred men and women from neighboring farms turned up for the meeting, most of them curious to find out what it was all about. Elizabeth Stanton presented a resolution that "it is the duty of the women of this country to secure to themselves the right of elective franchise."

If it hadn't been for that bold public demand for woman's right to vote the little village meeting probably would have been ignored. But newspapers in New York and Philadelphia and then other cities picked up the story of the "Insurrection Among Women." Male editorial writers and humorists had great sport making fun of "ladies who want to vote and hold public office while men put on petticoats to nurse the babies or preside at the wash tub."

Elizabeth Stanton and her friends didn't enjoy the ridicule but she was willing to be laughed at in exchange for "the publicity given to our ideas" and she predicted: "It will start women thinking, and men too, and when men and women think about a new question the first step in progress is taken."

All the controversy started some women thinking in nearby Rochester, New York, and that same year they held a woman's rights convention there that once again brought male ridicule but also enormous publicity. Soon, without any central direction, new groups began to spring up almost everywhere, with statewide meetings in Ohio, Indiana, Pennsylvania and Kansas.

More than one thousand delegates from places as distant as California crowded into Worcester, Massachusetts, in October, 1850, for the first National Woman's Rights Convention. A central committee was organized to produce literature and help plan other conventions and resolutions were adopted that "women are clearly entitled to the right of suffrage" and that "political rights acknowledge no sex and therefore the word 'male' should be stricken from every state constitution."

After that national conventions were held every year, state conventions were so frequent there was one somewhere every few months, and there were hundreds of smaller gatherings to swell the talk of woman's rights. Among those attracted to the movement was Susan B. Anthony, who had moved as a child with her Quaker family from Massachusetts to Rochester, New York, and who was a teacher and head of a girls' academy before she met Elizabeth Stanton and became a woman suffrage crusader.

She was a frequent visitor to the Stanton home in Seneca Falls and they became close friends and partners who planned together, wrote together, shared speaking platforms and drew up hundreds of resolutions, protests, appeals and petitions. Although there were many others who helped lead the movement, they became the driving force of its early years. Elizabeth Stanton was its philosopher and writer and Susan Anthony the one who brought it organization and political strength.

Hundreds of women were to devote a good part of their lives to the battle and they raised millions of dollars to support it through various suffrage associations. The Civil War brought a temporary halt to suffrage drives, but during the half-century that followed women organized nearly five hundred campaigns to try to change the voting laws of the states. They carried the fight into state and national political conventions, made it an issue in presidential elections, and in Washington sought action from nineteen congresses on a constitutional amendment for nationwide voting rights.

Yet the first small victory came without the help of the national associations. It was entirely a local effort by some pioneering women of the West. They quietly convinced the leaders of the first legislature of the new Territory of Wyoming that women who shared the dangers, labors and hardships of the frontier with their men deserved to share in its government.

Without petitions or any organized campaign the women of Wyoming became the first in the modern world to win the unlimited right to vote. There was some opposition but no great excitement as the territorial legislature finally passed the bill by a three-vote majority. It was signed into law December 10, 1869, and when Wyoming later applied for statehood woman suffrage was written into its new constitution.

Suffragists were a long time winning another victory in the states. In Washington their petitions to congress for nationwide voting rights by constitutional amendment were treated as a joke. It wasn't until 1878 that Susan Anthony managed to win the first senate committee hearing on the proposed amendment introduced for her that year by Senator Aaron Sargent of California, which simply and directly declared: "The right of citizens of the United States to vote shall not be denied or abridged by the United States or any state on account of sex."

What became known as the "Anthony Amendment" remained unchanged in its wording during the forty-two more years it was to take before it finally was made part of the constitution. In 1878 Elizabeth Stanton headed the women witnesses who argued for it before the Senate Committee on Privileges and Elections, whose members treated her with what she called "studied inattention and contempt." They stretched their arms, yawned in her face, stared at the ceiling, wandered away to sharpen pencils, and otherwise made it clear that the amendment had no chance of getting past the committee.

The suffragists had it introduced again at the next session of congress, and at every session after that, and hearings in one house or the other at least kept the issue alive in the newspapers. Gradually they also gained more support among members of congress. In 1882 both branches of congress appointed select committees and both favorably reported. Two years later and again in 1886 senate committees repeated their favorable reports, and the proposed amendment finally reached the senate floor for debate.

Hopes were high on January 25, 1887, when the Senate voted on woman suffrage for the first time. But the result was a crushing defeat. The Senate rejected it by a vote of more than two to one. For more than a quarter of a century, the Senate refused to vote on it again.

When they recovered from the blow the women reorganized their forces. They brought together two long-divided national groups and merged them in 1890 into a new National American Woman Suffrage Association pledged to a renewed battle in the states. Their goal was the winning of rights state by state until women voters had enough real political strength to force congress to recognize their demand for a constitutional amendment.

They turned again to the Far West. In Colorado in 1893 the woman suffrage question was put to the voters in a special referendum. Chosen to lead the battle there was Carrie Chapman Catt, long active in state suffrage campaigns. She had been an Iowa school principal and then a newspaper reporter in San Francisco before deciding to devote her life to the cause of woman's rights, and soon would head the national association when Susan Anthony retired. Carrie Chapman Catt's successful campaign in Colorado brought women their first state victory since Wyoming.

Utah and Idaho were the next to give women the vote, in 1896. After that fourteen years of battling in the states brought only defeat. But in 1910, after twice rejecting woman suffrage, the state of Washington was won over to it. Within two more years the big state of California, and then Oregon, Arizona and Kansas accepted women as voters. The tide rolled across the Mississippi in 1913 and the women of Illinois gained the vote in municipal, county and presidential elections.

The movement had grown strong, with influential supporters in state and national governments, with intelligently planned and well-financed political strategy, and with an increasing effect on public opinion everywhere. Up and down the country, suffragists were marching in parades through city streets, touring smaller towns in automobile caravans, flooding the press and magazines with their arguments, putting up billboards, staging pageants, plays, school essay contests, speaking from theater stages, street platforms, and soap boxes at factory gates.

But all of it had not yet changed the minds of the men in the Congress of the United States. The proposed constitutional amendment for woman suffrage had not moved in congress since 1887, buried in committee hearings that droned on annually like respectful services for the dead.

10

E<small>IGHT</small> <small>THOUSAND</small> <small>WOMEN</small> with suffrage banners flying paraded along Washington's Pennsylvania Avenue on March 3, 1913, the day before Woodrow Wilson's inauguration, to make the incoming president and congress aware of their cause. It was a parade that turned into a confrontation and near riot. Police had given a permit for it, but they did little to protect the women when angry men began attacking the marchers.

Women were slapped, tripped, spat upon, pelted with burning cigar stubs, had banners torn from their hands. Their hats were pulled off, their clothing was ripped, and some were knocked to the ground and trampled. Federal troops had to be called in from nearby Fort Meyer. The soldiers cleared the streets, controlled the mob, and finally restored order, and the somewhat disheveled women carried on with the parade that got them a lot more front-page attention than they had expected.

Behind the march that signaled the start of a militant new battle for a constitutional amendment was Alice Paul who, as a young American college graduate and social worker in London, had joined the fighting ranks of Brit-

74

ain's suffragettes. She had fought angry mobs there, staged street demonstrations, led protest marches on Parliament, had broken up government meetings and created other happenings to dramatize the suffrage cause. Another American girl, Lucy Burns, had shared some of her ordeals, including terms in English prisons where they went on hunger strikes to gain sympathy and headlines.

They came back to the United States and convinced the National Suffrage Association that some of the tactics they had learned in England could be used to put new life into the all but dead fight for a constitutional amendment. In Washington, Alice Paul set up a new Congressional Union for Woman Suffrage with the single goal of compelling congress to act. They meant to use any and every means they could to keep constant pressure on congress and the president and at the same time stir up nationwide protest that would flow in upon Washington from people in every congressional district.

Within a year the Congressional Union had organized women in every state and had raised thousands of dollars to support the fight in Washington by lobbying everywhere, not for state voting rights that had to be painfully won by slow-moving methods, but for one concentrated effort to win women the constitutional right to vote.

Large delegations of women were brought to Washington to visit the White House and plead with President Wilson and to visit the offices of congressmen from their various states. Floods of personal letters, telegrams, resolutions and petitions poured in upon senators and representatives from their home areas. In cities and villages from New York to California there were mass meetings by groups representing housewives, club women, women of industry, business and the professions. Wherever the president traveled or any congressman went, other delegations appeared. To project the image of the 20th Century Woman who deserved full equality with men, suffragists took part in cross-country automobile races and staged other publicity stunts.

Some older women found the new methods too radical, and others who had devoted their lives to suffrage work believed political power through voting rights in the states was still vital and that congress and the president could be better influenced by persuasion than by force. There was a break between Alice Paul's Congressional Union and the national association headed by Carrie Chapman Catt and they became separate organiations, each working in its own way in Washington and the states. Both achieved results that combined the direct pressure in Washington with increasing power in the states, and both were needed.

For the first time since it was defeated in 1887, woman suffrage was brought to a vote in the Senate on March 17, 1914. Thirty-five senators voted for it and thirty-four against, but the one-vote majority in its favor was far short of the two-thirds necessary to adopt a constitutional amendment. In the House, where it had never been brought to a vote, all action remained stalled by Democratic leaders who maintained that woman suffrage was "a state and not a national issue."

Since the Democrats were the party in power, Alice Paul's Congressional Union called upon American women to forget their own party affiliations and work to defeat Democratic candidates for congress in states where women had won the right to vote. Funds were raised and teams of organizers were sent out from Washington to nine western suffrage states to campaign against Democrats.

Some women were bitterly opposed to the drive, especially members of the old national association which had always been strictly non-partisan in attempting to win friends in both political parties. But when the November election returns were in the battling suffragists claimed at least partial credit for the defeat of twenty-three Democrats and for whittling down the majorities of some others who came back to congress. They had also broken the congressional deadlock.

On January 12, 1915, for the first time, the House voted on national woman suffrage. It was defeated 204 to 174 but many were surprised that it showed that much strength. The goal had been to force the proposed amendment to the floor of both houses of congress, whatever its chances of passing, thus bringing it back to life, and that much the women had done.

President Wilson, despite the pressure upon him from the day he entered the White House, was reluctant at first to support the amendment. Personally he believed women should have the right to vote but he also believed they should gain that right from the individual states and not from the federal government.

As leader of the Democratic party, the traditional champion of state's rights, he felt states alone should have the power to decide who could vote and that amending the constitution would amount to dictating to the states. In the end he became convinced the amendment was the only way women could gain their full citizenship and he put all the prestige of the presidency behind it, but not until he had been brought to that decision one slow step at a time.

In the close election of 1916, with the presidency, the entire membership of the House and one-third of the Senate at stake, some suffragists attempted to form an independent Woman's Party in the twelve states where they had voting rights, but without much practical success. Others sought action through the established political parties.

Thousands of women marched in demonstrations at the Republican and Democratic National Conventions. The Republicans, for the first time, included woman suffrage in their platform, but the wording of the resolution was disappointingly indefinite. The Democrats, to the booing protest of women in the gallery, adopted a platform plank favoring suffrage by state action, not constitutional amendment.

When President Wilson was reelected in November, 1916, along with many of the Democrats in Congress who had always opposed woman suffrage, Alice Paul decided the time had come for more militant action. In January, 1917, the first of hundreds of suffragists began to picket the White House, determined to stand "at the President's gate day by day, week in and week out" for however long it took to embarrass him before the nation and the world with a dramatic demand for woman's political liberty that neither he nor the congress could ignore.

Included in the marchers, who changed ranks every few hours, were working women, school teachers, college students, women lawyers and doctors, wives of prominent government officials, even a grandmother of eighty. Nobody tried to interfere with them at first. President Wilson smiled tolerantly and waved to them as he was driven out of the White House grounds past banners that asked: "Mr. President—How Long Must Women Wait For Liberty?"

When the United States entered the First World War and President Wilson called for a world "made safe for democracy," the pickets hoisted signs that said, "Democracy Begins At Home!" and "Help Us Make Our Own Nation Free!" But crowds of men, inflamed by wartime patriotism and deeply resentful of the White House picketing which they considered an insult both to the president and the nation, began to jeer at the women and finally there were scuffles and attempts to tear down the signs.

Washington police moved in and started arresting the pickets on charges of "obstructing traffic." As fast as they made arrests more pickets appeared and more arrests were made. The women accused President Wilson and his administration of trying to suppress their civil liberties by force. Found guilty of "creating a nuisance" by blocking the sidewalk in front of the White House, the suffragists refused to pay small fines and were put in jail.

Violence grew as the picketing continued. Within weeks more than two hundred women had been arrested. The courts gradually increased their sentences from a few days in jail to prison terms of six months or more. Many of those arrested were hurried over to the Occoquan workhouse in nearby Virginia, where they were put into prison uniforms, denied counsel and contact with friends outside, and were forced to perform rough prison labor. Some whom authorities branded "trouble-makers" were put in solitary confinement and others became ill from physical mistreatment and a diet that later testimony revealed consisted mainly of "sour bread and rancid soups."

President Wilson was shocked by private reports of the mistreatment that reached him and for a time arrests were halted, but the picketing went on, there was renewed violence, and new arrests were made. None of the women was ever charged with any serious crime. The only legal pretense for imprisoning them was that they were obstructing the White House sidewalk. When details of their punishment leaked out to the newspapers and sensational news stories appeared many prominent Americans joined in demanding a full investigation and people in all parts of the country began bombarding their congressmen with letters and telegrams of protest.

The president finally ordered all the arrested pickets unconditionally released from jail. Months later the District of Columbia Court of Appeals ruled that every one of the jailed women had been illegally arrested, illegally convicted and illegally imprisoned. The picketing, arrests, widespread public indignation and publicity and sympathy for the suffragists had its political effect in congress and on an administration that became anxious to do something to satisfy the nation's women and put an end to the hue and cry that had been carried to the White House gates.

But it wasn't the picketing alone that changed the climate in favor of the woman suffrage amendment. While Alice Paul's militant suffragists were demonstrating in Washington the national suffrage association under Carrie Chapman Catt's leadership had followed opposite tactics. Making it clear that they had no part in the attempts to attack the Democrats politically or in the picketing to embarrass the president, they had kept their own door to the White House open, seeking to persuade President Wilson to cooperate and support the amendment.

Backed by some two million members across the country, the association had been hard at work winning the right to vote in key states that would give women added political power when the amendment came to a showdown in congress, and the state battles came to a turning point in 1917. During the early months of the year six more states were added to those which granted some form of suffrage to their women. That November, after sixty years of campaigning, a massive effort finally brought victory in the politically vital state of New York.

President Wilson at last declared himself in favor of the amendment "as an act of right and justice to the women of the country." He publicly urged congress to support it the day before it came to a vote in the House of Representatives on January 10, 1918.

With every vote needed, several congressmen who supported woman suffrage made a wild dash across the country from their homes on the Pacific Coast to arrive just in time to cast their ballots. Four others left hospital sickbeds to vote and Representative Harry Barnhart of Indiana was carried into the House chamber on a stretcher.

The House passed the amendment 272 to 136, exactly the necessary two-thirds majority. Watching from the gallery, some suffragists cheered and others wept in the belief that after years of battle the struggle was all but won. They soon learned they were wrong. The Senate was not about to go along with the House in quickly approving the amendment. Opponents in the Senate fought through all of 1918 and half the next year to kill it if they could.

President Wilson, having taken his stand for it, used his full influence in attempts to break the senate deadlock by calling key senators to the White House for private conferences. When the Senate finally agreed to let it come to a vote, certain it would be defeated, the president dramatically carried his appeal right into the senate chamber. With only a half-hour's notice to the Senate, where the debate was already underway, he intervened by appearing in person to urge immediate passage of the amendment as a war measure.

The people of the world were "looking to the great, powerful, famous democracy of the West to lead them to the new day" in which democracy would mean "that women shall play their part in affairs alongside men and upon an equal footing with them," the president said. "We have made partners of the women in this war; shall we admit them only to a partnership of sacrifice and suffering and toil, and not to a partnership of privilege and right?"

But the day after he appeared the Senate defeated the amendment by a narrow margin of two votes short of the two-thirds majority needed to pass it. Again, in February, 1919, the Senate defeated it by one vote. Women meanwhile gained voting rights in three additional states and they also increased their strength among newly-elected members of congress.

With the war over President Wilson was about to bring the peace treaty back from Paris and in a cabled message calling the new congress into special session he once more urged passage of the woman suffrage amendment. The House repassed it immediately by a sweeping majority but the Senate still delayed.

At last, on June 4, 1919, the debate which had gone on in congress for more than forty years ended. Senate die-hards fought to the end, until Senator Robert La Follette of Wisconsin gained the floor and made a speech that consisted of only one word. He said, "Vote!" By a vote of 66 to 30 the Senate agreed to submit the 19th Amendment to the Constitution for ratification by the states.

Even then, there was doubt. By August, 1919, fourteen states had ratified, with Wisconsin winning honors as the first, but after that it took another full year of battling in the states. In each state there were campaigns, parades, demonstrations and political maneuvering to fight down the desperate opposition of those determined to kill the amendment. With thirty-five states won, the last struggle centered upon Tennessee in the summer of 1920.

It took a United States Supreme Court ruling and a personal plea from President Wilson to overcome a Tennessee law and bring the legislature into special session. At one point, in an attempt to block action, nearly half the members of the legislature hurried across the state line at midnight to absent themselves from Tennessee.

But Tennessee became the thirty-sixth state to ratify and at eight-o'clock on the morning of August 26, 1920, Secretary of State Bainbridge Colby, who had waited up all night in his Washington office to receive the official ratification certificate, signed the proclamation of the woman suffrage amendment.

Women everywhere marched in victory parades. In New

York, after a giant celebration, Carrie Chapman Catt said, "I have lived to realize the great dream of my life—the enfranchisement of women. We are no longer petitioners, we are not the wards of the nation, but free and equal citizens."

That fall of 1920, when millions of women registered for the first nationwide elections in which they would have a voice, she reminded them that the right to vote had "cost millions of dollars and the lives of thousands of women" and she wrote: "Women have suffered an agony of soul which you can never comprehend, that you and your daughters might inherit political freedom. That vote has been costly. *Prize it!*"

11

For the negro, winning the constitutional right to vote was only the beginning of his struggle for voting freedom. In America's early years, when the right to vote was restricted to free men of property, some free blacks who could meet the necessary requirements voted equally with free whites. But free Negroes were comparatively few and the hundreds of thousands who were slaves were never allowed to vote.

Even the small number who had gained their freedom found it difficult to exercise their legal right, which the states soon began to take away from them. Georgia and South Carolina from the time of the Revolution had limited suffrage to white males. Between 1792 and 1838 the constitutions of Connecticut, Delaware, Kentucky, Maryland, New Jersey, North Carolina, Tennessee and Virginia were changed to exclude all Negroes from voting, despite their proclamations of equal rights for all men. With the sole exception of Maine, every new state that entered the Union between 1800 and the eve of the Civil War denied blacks the right to vote.

By the time the Civil War began they could vote only

in New York, if they could meet special taxpayer and property qualifications there, and in the five New England states of Maine, New Hampshire, Vermont, Rhode Island and Massachusetts, where there were no specific color lines for suffrage but where only about six percent of America's Negroes lived. Elsewhere in the United States no black man, slave or free, could vote.

From the very start of the anti-slavery movement many abolitionists, black and white, had argued that equal suffrage would have to follow any freeing of the slaves if they were to remain truly free. Agitation grew through the years of Civil War, as the war itself changed from what began as a Northern struggle to put down rebellion and became a moral crusade to end slavery. But the Emancipation Proclamation and even the coming of peace brought no assurance to the Negro of the right to vote.

President Lincoln's plan for restoring the former slave states to the Union called for recognition of new state governments formed by voters who swore loyalty to the United States and who pledged to support all acts of congress and presidential proclamations "with reference to slaves." But the qualification of voters was to be based on "the election law of the state existing immediately before the so-called act of secession," which meant government by whites only.

Succeeding him as president, Andrew Johnson closely followed Lincoln's plan of restoration and hurried the reunion of the Southern states by presidential proclamations that recognized new governments as quickly as they could be formed. But his policy of broad conciliation toward the South, and his insistence on minimum federal interference with the right of the states to remake their own governments, brought no suffrage to the newly-freed slaves.

Ten Southern states during 1865 and 1866 held organizing conventions or legislative sessions and not one even extended the vote to Negroes on a limited basis or seriously considered doing so. The new governments brought back to state power many of the same men who had held it during the Confederacy. They enacted codes of law to control the blacks who had been set free, so-called "Black Codes" that restricted nearly all civil rights and personal liberties.

In Washington the reaction in congress was almost immediate. The first Civil Rights Act, designed to protect the freed slaves from such discriminating laws as the Black Codes, was passed over President Johnson's veto on April 9, 1866. It was the first federal law to define citizenship and to attempt to extend federal protection to civil rights within the states.

It declared that citizens "of every race and color, without regard to any previous condition of slavery," were to have the same right in every state and territory "to full and equal benefit of all laws . . . as is enjoyed by white citizens." Anyone convicted of violating the Civil Rights Act could be fined or imprisoned. The president was empowered to enforce it through the use of federal troops if necessary. But President Johnson, who had denounced it as dangerously unconstitutional, had no intention of using such powers. He also disagreed with those who argued that since Negroes were citizens that automatically gave them a "natural right" to vote.

The Radical wing of the Republican party in congress soon was in open rebellion against President Johnson. For political as well as moral reasons its leaders meant to create hundreds of thousands of new black voters in the South to strengthen the Republican party nationally and to prevent any rebirth of the once-dominant Southern Democrats. The Republican Radicals asserted that congress alone had authority to decide when states should be readmitted to the Union. What President Johnson had done they considered nothing less than a disaster.

When President Johnson proclaimed the all but complete reorganization of the former Confederate states and their restoration to the Union, congress totally rejected it. Congress refused to recognize the credentials of the states and refused to seat the congressmen they had sent to Washington.

A joint House and Senate Committee on Reconstruction reported that the "so-called Confederate states" remained "disorganized communities" that were without "the sanction of the people." Congress, the committee decided, would not be justified "in admitting such communities to a participation in the government of the country without first providing such constitutional . . . guarantees as will tend to secure the civil rights of all citizens of the republic."

The congressional Radicals intended to write the principals of the first Civil Rights Act into the constitution to protect it from attack in the courts or possible repeal by some future congress. Out of weeks of committee hearings came the proposed 14th Amendment, a great landmark in assuring basic rights to all Americans.

The amendment translated into law the concept that America was no longer just a grouping of states but a nation bound together so that the common citizenship of its people extended to all the states. All persons who were born or naturalized Americans, it said, were citizens not only of the state where they lived but also citizens of the entire United States, and the federal government would guarantee protection of those basic rights of common citizenship against invasion by any individual state.

It gave constitutional status to full citizenship for the Negro and its supporters hoped it also would influence the states to grant Negro suffrage. But in order to get it through the opposition in congress, they backed away from writing into the amendment any language that would directly give the vote to blacks.

As a substitute for an outright grant of suffrage they added a second section to the proposed amendment which they thought would be a potent weapon to compel the Southern states to act. It threatened to reduce the number of representatives a state could have in congress in proportion to the number of Negro citizens of that state who were denied a right to vote. But it was a threat that was never used. Although finally written into the constitution, it was allowed to die there, never enforced by congress or the courts despite attempts over the years to revive it.

When the 14th Amendment was offered for ratification to all thirty-six states including those in the South, congress let it be understood that it spelled out the basic terms under which it would readmit the seceded states to the Union. Tennessee was the only Southern state that ratified it at first and was readmitted. Ten other former Confederate states rejected it and their presidentially restored governments were put out of existence.

The Republican Radicals, swept back into congress in overwhelming strength in the fall elections of 1866, threw the armed force of the federal government behind the immediate securing of Negro rights, especially voting rights. The Radicals took command of a congress that assumed nearly dictatorial power over all other branches of government and hammered out their own forced reconstruction of the South.

Over President Johnson's protest that "the Federal government has no jurisdiction, authority or power . . . to force the right of suffrage out of the hands of the white people and into the hands of the Negroes," congress early in 1867 enacted the first of a series of Reconstruction Acts. Declaring that "no legal state governments now exist in the rebel states," it divided the South into five military districts where federal troops and military courts would enforce the "protection of all persons in their rights" until "loyal and republican governments can be legally established."

Negroes would have to be given a full voice in forming any new state government. They would have to be admitted to suffrage at elections for delegates to a convention to frame the government and write its new constitution. The state constitution would have to guarantee Negroes the permanent right to vote. It could be ratified only if they were among the voters who decided whether to accept it. Even then state constitutions would have to be submitted to congress for examination and approval. Each of the states would also have to ratify the 14th Amendment.

Only when all such conditions required by the Reconstruction Acts had been met would congress decide whether to readmit any state to the Union and whether to seat its senators and representatives. Until then all civil government within any military district would remain "subject to the paramount authority of the United States at any time to abolish, modify, control or supersede."

Backed by a force of some 20,000 soldiers, the Union commanders of the military districts carried out the political will of congress. By the end of 1867, under Army rule, about 700,000 Southern blacks had been registered as voters, along with a slightly smaller number of qualified whites who had taken an oath of loyalty to the Union. Under military protection they joined in choosing delegates to form new state governments and in electing officials to run them. Working together under watchful federal supervision, blacks and whites rapidly brought the new states into being.

The Radicals in congress were not satisfied with the indirect protection the 14th Amendment gave Negro suffrage. They feared that when federal troops eventually were withdrawn the Southern states might repeal the voting rights secured only by military force. To block that possibility, congress decided a more drastic constitutional amendment was needed. The result was the proposed 15th Amendment, which provided that: "The right of citizens of the United States to vote shall not be denied or abridged by the United States or by any state on account of race, color or previous condition of servitude."

By the time it was ratified in 1870 all the reconstructed Southern states had been readmitted to the Union, with Negro members of the new legislatures playing a large part in the process. While they never actually controlled any of the Radical governments except by political cooperation with white Republicans, blacks sometimes made the majority in one branch of a legislature. No Negro was elected governor of any Southern state during the Reconstruction years but three were elected lieutenant-governors and many served in other high state offices. Southern Radicals sent fourteen Negroes to Washington as representatives and two as senators.

Whites continued to dominate Southern state governments during the entire period, but not as they had when the South was a stronghold of the Democratic party and of absolute white supremacy. The Reconstruction governments were mainly controlled by white Republicans who shared power with the new black Republicans, to the outrage of the South's traditional ruling class.

Even with military protection many Negro voters had been intimidated and cheated of their votes. Hours of election and the location of polling places were changed without notice. Ballots were issued with names of candidates missing and ballot boxes vanished and votes were stolen. Blacks were warned to vote as they were told to vote or they would lose jobs, be forced to work on road gangs, or be forced back into slavery. Others were ordered to stay home or be shot.

As violence and intimidation grew it became more organized. Secret orders such as the Ku Klux Klan and other groups of white "redeemers" planned and carried out the systematic terrorizing of black voters and their white Republican supporters. The Klan, the largest of the terrorist bands, asked those taken into its secret membership to swear that they were "opposed to Negro equality, both social and political" and that they favored "a white man's government."

Hooded midnight raiders on fast horses, carefully choosing their victims for attack to spread fear through a selected area, burned homes, barns and crops, and whipped, clubbed, shot and murdered. They issued printed and verbal warnings that others would suffer the same fate if they dared to vote, hold meetings or encourage the political independence of blacks.

Determined to destroy the enforced power of the Republican party and restore the South to the Democrats and white supremacy, armed whites took over some towns on election day and "drove the colored men before them and compelled them to fly for their lives," according to testimony given a congressional investigating committee. In Louisiana during the presidential election of 1868 reportedly "half the state was overrun by violence, midnight raids, secret murders and open riot" which "kept the people in constant terror until Republicans surrendered all claims."

Congress in 1871 collected thirteen volumes of testimony on violence and fraud in Southern elections and passed laws to ban terrorist groups and to impose stiff penalties for interfering with Negro voters. But a series of Supreme Court decisions drew the teeth from most of the laws and federal enforcement slackened. With the formation of accepted state governments, military control was lifted from some areas. Local authorities, often under the influence of the Klan or other secret groups, seldom arrested suspected terrorists and courts and juries almost never convicted them.

Republicans in the North, no longer aflame with Radical

zeal, had become the party of big business whose conservative leaders were finding they had less in common with the blacks and "poor whites" who were Southern Republicans than with the South's old ruling class of conservative Democrats. Many other Northerners, anxious to forget the bitterness of the war and to promote business and industrial expansion, were willing to accept compromises that promised to restore "political stability" to the South. Protests against the mistreatment of Negro voters were less vigorous.

Driven from the polls, harassed and cheated, blacks gradually were forced out of political power and white supremacists began to reclaim control of the Southern states. The takeover by white Democrats was an all but accomplished fact by the time the "stolen election" of 1876 put Republican Rutherford B. Hayes into the White House and brought the final compromise that ended Reconstruction.

Hayes lacked the votes to become president unless the returns from South Carolina, Louisiana and Florida were counted in his favor against Democrat Samuel J. Tilden who had been chosen president by an overwhelming majority of the nation's voters. Republican election boards, supported by federal troops still stationed in those states, managed to produce one set of returns claiming victory for Hayes, but Democratic officials in the contested states produced a second set of returns to show Tilden the winner.

With congress politically deadlocked over which votes to count, nobody knew who would be president for four months after the election and fear grew that the nation might be plunged into rioting, anarchy or a second Civil

War. Conservatives on both sides, alarmed by the public uproar and drawn together by their desire to put an end to the conflicts that still divided North and South and that were hurting the business prosperity of both, held a series of secret meetings and reached an agreement. Leading Southern Democrats met with Hayes' Republican managers in a Washington hotel room and made a deal.

When an electoral commission dominated by Republicans finally maneuvered the returns to give the presidency to Hayes by one electoral vote, the Southern Democrats broke their own party's opposition, accepted Hayes as president, and cleared the way for his inauguration.

Their price was a pledge from Hayes to remove remaining federal troops from the South, to end Reconstruction and all Northern "interference" with self-rule in the South, and to give them a free hand in taking over the Southern states not already reclaimed. Hayes kept the bargain. As soon as he became president in 1877 he ordered the last federal troops withdrawn.

With the departure of the last military forces, federal protection of Negro voting equality in the South became a paper promise. The Civil War had freed the blacks from physical slavery but their brief taste of self-government was gone. The Southern states rapidly completed the Negro's return to political slavery.

Blacks still had the constitution's guarantee of their right to vote equally with whites but where they weren't driven away from the polls by force or by other methods that denied the effectiveness of their votes, they were allowed to vote only in support of whites who had regained control. In exchange for such support some Negroes continued to hold offices, distributed by white politicians on the basis of black votes delivered to them.

During the 1870's and 1880's controlled Negro votes were important in the struggles between the Southern Democratic party and its Populist and Farmer Alliance opponents. Bitterly at odds, white factions used Negro votes against each other, but despite their wide political differences the whites eventually joined in a determination to exclude the blacks entirely.

They found less violent methods to eliminate Negro voting by state laws that had the practical effect of insuring government by whites only. Without obviously violating the constitution in their wording the carefully drawn laws evaded it, and the Southern states effectively nullified the 15th Amendment.

Rebuffed, discouraged, forbidden to support any candidates except those who enforced white supremacy, more and more blacks simply abandoned their efforts to vote. Nationally, Negro suffrage was an almost lost crusade, until a people began to fight again for a right that had been given and then taken away.

12

By THE START of the 20th Century all eleven former Confederate states had made it almost impossible for most Negroes to vote in the South, despite the 15th Amendment, by creating devious state election laws that admitted white voters and kept out blacks.

When Mississippi called a convention in 1890 to write a new state constitution delegates candidly declared its purpose was to restrict the black vote and to secure "supremacy of the white race," and they brewed a formula of discrimination to accomplish those aims by enacting a poll tax and a literacy test.

One delegate hoped the poll tax would have the same effect as saying to Mississippi's impoverished blacks, "We will give you two dollars not to vote." Payment of the tax was required months before election day and written receipts, difficult to obtain, had to be shown by the would-be voter.

The literacy test required all applicants for voter registration to give a "reasonable interpretation" of a section of the constitution. Most blacks in Mississippi as well as some whites could neither read nor write, but since it was up to each white election official to decide for himself who passed the test, blacks could be rejected and whites accepted. Even highly educated Negroes could be turned away by testing them on sections of the constitution few lawyers could interpret easily while illiterate whites were given simple passages to explain.

Mississippi's new laws had a quick and lasting effect. Within two years after they were adopted, Negro registration in the state, which previously had included almost seventy percent of those of voting age, fell to less than six percent. Between 1895 and 1910 other Southern states set up similar qualifications for voting. They varied from state to state but had the same result: the elimination of Negroes as voters. Some states included vague tests of "good character" or "civic understanding" as well as stiff residency and property qualifications.

White voters in a number of states were exempted from literacy tests by so-called "grandfather clauses," which allowed them to vote if their ancestors had voted in the years before Reconstruction even though they themselves otherwise might not be qualified to vote. Other alternatives were provided to assure that whites were not disfranchised while blacks were.

The Southern purpose was summed up in 1898 by the president of Louisiana's state constitutional convention, which had just adopted the "grandfather clause," poll taxes and other voter restrictions, when he told the delegates: "We have not drafted the exact constitution that we should like to have drafted; otherwise we should have inserted in it . . . the exclusion from the suffrage of every man with a trace of African blood in his veins . . ." But he asked, "Doesn't it meet the case? Doesn't it let the white man vote and doesn't it stop the Negro from voting, and isn't that what we came here for?"

Two years before Louisiana wrote its new constitution there had been 130,000 blacks registered to vote in the state, but two years afterwards the total had dwindled to only 5,000. Within another four years, by 1904, black voters in all of Louisiana had been reduced to a mere 1,342.

Even if a Negro somehow managed to get past all the legal barriers and become a registered voter, his vote was made worthless by what soon proved an even more potent means of disfranchising him, the use of primary elections by the ruling Democratic party to allow only whites to vote for candidates.

The Republican party, which to most Southern whites symbolized the hated years of Reconstruction and the attempt to force Negro suffrage upon them, was reduced to insignificant strength and in many Southern localities all but disappeared. For at least fifty years, from the end of Reconstruction into the 1940's, the Democratic party was absolutely dominant in the states of the old Confederacy.

That meant that whoever was nominated by the party's voters in the Democratic primary was as good as elected, since the general election that followed would almost automatically put into office the Democratic candidates already chosen in the primary. Under laws adopted by most of the Southern states political parties were allowed to set their own rules for membership which gave them the power to keep Negroes from voting in the party's primary.

Democratic party committees simply decided that Negroes could not be Democrats and by barring them from party membership denied them any voice in nominating candidates. A Negro, if he were a registered voter, could still cast a ballot in the general election, but it was an empty gesture since the white primary had already decided who would be elected. For all practical purposes the election was over before Negroes could take part in it.

The Supreme Court, in a series of rulings between 1927 and 1935, at first tried to draw a line between what a state could do and what Democratic committees could do, acting as individuals. The Court, in various decisions, held that it was unconstitutional to bar Negroes from a primary by specific state law but refused to interfere if a state removed all racial qualifications from its law and let the parties decide who could vote in primaries. The reasoning was that a political party was like a golf club or any other private club that had a right to decide who to admit to membership.

Finally, in 1944, the Court outlawed the white primary altogether in a landmark decision that overturned the legal doctrines which for nearly half a century had supported the South's "most formidable barrier" to Negro voting. The case of *Smith v. Allwright* grew out of a suit by a Texas Negro, Lonnie Smith, against an election official of that state who had refused to give him a ballot in a primary election for the nomination of congressional candidates.

The Court reversed itself, overruled previous decisions, and decided that whatever a political party did was done by ultimate authority of the state. The primary election, the Court held, was not a private matter but part of the state's machinery for choosing officials, carried out in conformity with state laws. Therefore the state had endorsed racial discrimination by a political party in violation of the 15th Amendment and the white primary was declared unconstitutional. Some states accepted the decision and some tried to find other means to evade it for a time, but later court tests also outlawed the evasions and the white primary finally was abandoned in the South.

Some of the other barriers to Negro voting gradually were knocked down by the slow process of years of legal skirmishing and by the activities of many groups and individuals intended to arouse public opinion. The poll tax came under increasingly heavy public and congressional attack, not only as a device to restrict Negro voting but because it discouraged voting in general, since states with poll taxes usually were those with the lowest voter participation by poor whites as well as blacks.

North Carolina dropped its poll tax in 1920, followed by Louisiana in 1934, Florida in 1937, and in later years by South Carolina and Tennessee. The Supreme Court and lower federal courts had held that the tax was a legitimate revenue measure, applied to all voters, and that it did not violate the constitution. But congressional hearings gave much publicity to abuses of the tax and public opinion grew behind demands for new federal legislation.

A Senate Judiciary Subcommittee issued a report in 1942 declaring that the poll tax laws in Southern states were "motivated entirely and exclusively by a desire to exclude the Negro from voting." But Southern filibusters or threats of them in the Senate killed every attempt in congress to legislate against poll taxes. Five times between 1942 and 1949, the House passed laws against the taxes and each time they died in the Senate.

Unable to outlaw the poll tax by act of congress, its opponents took another route and sought to change the constitution itself by amendment. But it wasn't until the summer of 1962 that the turning point in poll tax reform finally came when Congress approved and sent to the states,
where it was ratified, the proposed 24th Amendment to
the constitution, which declared:

"The right of citizens of the United States to vote in
any primary or other election for President or Vice-President . . . or for Senator or Representatives in Congress
shall not be denied or abridged by the United States or
any State by reason of failure to pay any poll tax or other
tax."

Only the states of Alabama, Arkansas, Mississippi, Texas
and Virginia, in the South, still had poll taxes the amendment could prohibit by the time it was ratified in 1964 and
made part of the constitution. However, the amendment
still left states free to impose a poll tax in elections for
state and local officials until the Supreme Court in 1966
dealt it a final blow. The Court voided the tax in state and
and local as well as in federal elections on the grounds that
it violated the equal protection clause of the 14th Amendment.

In the long battle against literacy tests less gain was
made in the courts. The Supreme Court repeatedly upheld
the right of states to require literacy tests if state law applied them equally to everybody. In 1915 the Court did
outlaw the "grandfather clause" which had let illiterate
whites with approved ancestors evade taking the tests
blacks had to take. But down through the years the Court
held to the position that the constitution did not prohibit

tests when state law authorized them without direct racial discrimination.

Justice Oliver Wendell Holmes, back in 1903 when the Supreme Court rejected one of the first challenges of the literacy tests that had disfranchised Alabama Negroes, advised the voteless blacks that the federal courts could offer only limited remedies and that in the long run they would have to look to the people for relief from such a "great political wrong."

In later years the Court's historic civil rights decisions were to change the whole climate of the nation's attitude toward Negro equality. But it was by their own power as voters that the people began to bring about the change. Their growing influence on congress and political leaders in Washington set in motion what eventually was to become a massive federal effort to assure Negro suffrage.

13

IT WAS OUTSIDE the South that Negroes first began to gain political strength. Since the days of Abraham Lincoln most American Negroes had remained Republicans, but city Negroes of the North began to vote as Democrats in the years of Franklin Roosevelt's New Deal. His revolutionary programs of social and economic change offered hope in the bitter depression to the "one-third of a nation" that was poor, which included most blacks, and they became among his strongest supporters.

President Roosevelt brought outstanding Negroes into high positions in the federal government, men and women who served as "racial advisers" to the many New Deal agencies. By 1939 his administration had created a Civil Rights Section in the Department of Justice, under Attorney General Frank Murphy, which was to "direct, supervise and conduct prosecutions of the provisions of the Constitution or Acts of Congress guaranteeing civil rights to individuals."

With limited manpower and not much support from congress, the new Civil Rights Section was only able to act on a small number of the thousands of complaints received.

But it did achieve significant court victories that provided government lawyers with much stronger legal ammunition for the voting rights battles that were to come.

The great exodus of blacks from the South into the cities of the North, that had begun as a flight for survival in the desperate years of depression, grew into an increasing migration of thousands during and after the Second World War. Settling in Northern and then Western manufacturing states from New York to California, they took an active interest in voting and in political organization. Negro vote power, especially in the big cities, became a force that influenced Northern politicians and gave new thrust to the whole movement for civil rights.

In the South as well as in the North, the Congress of Racial Equality, National Association for the Advancement of Colored People, and other groups of blacks and liberal whites quickened the battle for greater civil rights. Encouraged by the Supreme Court decision that had outlawed the white primary and by decisions in other courts that began to knock down some of the barriers to voting, Negro registration throughout the South quadrupled between 1940 and 1947 to nearly 600,000.

But the gain still was only a small percentage of the potential Negro voters in the South. In Alabama and Mississippi only an estimated one percent of blacks of voting age, and only two percent in Louisiana, were registered as voters by 1947. In four Southern states less than fifteen percent were registered, and in no Southern state were there more than twenty-five percent registered to vote.

President Harry Truman called for a change in public policy in 1947. "There is much that state and local governments can do in providing positive safeguards for civil rights. But we cannot, any longer, await the growth of a will to action in the slowest state or the most backward community," he said. "Our national government must show the way."

He established a President's Committee on Civil Rights to study the problem and to recommend federal action. In 1948, as the elections of that year made civil rights an issue that divided Northern and Southern Democrats, Truman became the first president to seek the full entry of the federal government into the civil rights field. He called on congress to enact a comprehensive program of legislation based on the recommendations of his advisory committee, but the congress failed to act.

In the absence of congressional action, the people acted, through the courts and in more direct and dramatic demonstrations. The Supreme Court's decision for school desegregation in 1954, followed by the Montgomery, Alabama, bus boycott and other events that kept the struggle for civil rights flaming in newspaper headlines, not only aroused public conscience but also made political leaders of both parties acutely sensitive to voter reaction.

By 1956 there was a rebirth in congress of concern for civil rights and especially for voting rights. Facing the voters that year, congressmen had to be concerned. A study by the *Congressional Quarterly* in April indicated that Negro voters might hold the balance of power in sixty-one congressional districts in twenty-one Northern and Western states. In the presidential race the influx of Negroes into highly urbanized industrial states might swing key contests that involved 212 of the 268 electoral votes required for presidential victory.

Even in the eleven Southern states the number of Negroes registered to vote had risen by 1956 to more than 1,238,000, although an estimated seventy-five percent of the nearly five million blacks of voting age in the South still were not registered voters.

When Republican President Dwight Eisenhower was reelected in November, 1956, the results showed that fifteen percent more Negroes had voted for him than four years before. The greatest shift to Eisenhower by any major population group had been by Negro Democrats in the North. To both political parties, Negro vote power had become significant and in congress some Democrats joined Republicans to give bipartisan support to the first federal protection of equal rights for Negroes since the Reconstruction era after the Civil War.

President Eisenhower had asked congress for legislation to enforce the guarantees written into the constitution and expounded by the Supreme Court. Attorney General Herbert Brownell, Jr., whose Department of Justice lawyers drafted the legislation, had argued at Eisenhower cabinet meetings and at congressional hearings in 1956 that protection of voting rights was a federal responsibility when states denied those rights.

Basically designed to help Negroes vote, the Civil Rights Act of 1957, which was hotly contested in both houses of congress, finally was guided through the Senate by Democrat Lyndon Johnson of Texas. It established a new Commission on Civil Rights as an independent fact-finding agency and expanded the old Civil Rights Section of the Justice Department into a full-fledged law enforcement division under a new assistant attorney general.

"No person, whether acting under the color of law or otherwise," the act declared, "shall intimidate, threaten, coerce, or attempt to intimidate . . . any other person for the purpose of interfering with the right of such other person to vote . . ."

The vindication of voting rights no longer would have to depend on court suits brought by individuals. Congress authorized the attorney general "in the name of the United States" to seek injunctions in federal district courts against anyone who tried to obstruct citizens in their right to vote.

Charges made by citizens that they had been deprived of the right to vote "by reason of their color, race, religion or national origin" would be investigated by the new Civil Rights Commission, with the power of court-enforced subpoena to summon reluctant witnesses to testify at hearings. Appointed by the president, the Commission also would study the legal devices used to evade constitutional protection of voting equality and would report on how well federal laws and policies were working to help congress plan additional legislation that might be needed.

Three years later some of the immediate gaps discovered in the new law were filled in by the Civil Rights Act of 1960, again put through congress with bipartisan support. Introduced by Senator Lyndon Johnson, about to become vice-president, the law also had the help of Senator John Kennedy of Massachusetts, who was about to become president.

The Act of 1960 prohibited voter registrars from concealing or destroying records when faced with investigation and allowed the attorney general to sue the state if local election officials suddenly resigned to evade court action. It also called for sending special court-appointed "voting referees" into districts where there was a proven "pattern or practice" of denying the vote to Negroes so that the referees could help federal courts enforce fair registration.

Kennedy, in the 1960 campaign, had pledged himself to a comprehensive new civil rights program that was blocked for a time by a hostile congress. As president he repeatedly urged congress to act, and took swift action himself to protect the right of Negro James Meredith to enter the University of Mississippi and to halt the violence that met crusades against the segregation of bus terminals and other public places in the Deep South.

By 1963, the one hundredth anniversary year of the Emancipation Proclamation, the whole nation was aroused by the crisis over civil rights that had brought massive demonstrations, terrorism, bombings, beatings and murder. Among those slain was Medgar Evers, leader of a Negro registration drive in Mississippi, who was shot to death at the doorway of his home. In August, more than 200,000 Americans of every age, sex, color and walk of life took part in one of the largest single protests in American history, the March on Washington, to dramatize their discontent over the continued denial of Negro rights.

The demand for all forms of civil freedoms had increased the voter education and registration activities of such organizations as the National Association for the Advancement of Colored People, the Congress of Racial Equality, the Southern Christian Leadership Conference, and the Student Nonviolent Coordinating Committee. Hundreds of college students and other young people from the North, black and white, spread through the South to join in the work of registering Negro voters.

The Kennedy administration had cleared the new civil rights legislation through the House Judiciary Committee but its ultimate fate in congress was still uncertain when, on November 22 in Dallas, John Kennedy was assassinated. Five days later in his first speech as president, to a joint session of congress and to the shocked nation, Lyndon Johnson said: "No memorial oration or eulogy could more eloquently honor President Kennedy's memory than the earliest possible passage of the civil rights bill for which he fought so long."

By the next February it had passed the House. But there were still delays, debates and threats to filibuster it to death in the Senate before it finally came through congress on July 2, 1964. President Johnson, who signed it into law the same day, said: "Those who are equal before God shall now also be equal in the polling booths, in the classrooms, in the factories, and in hotels, restaurants, movie theaters and other places that provide service to the public."

The Act of 1964 covered a broad range of purposes. Among them it gave federal district courts jurisdiction to issue injunctions against discrimination in public accommodations and public education. The act extended the Commission on Civil Rights, prohibited discrimination in programs assisted by federal funds, and established a Commission on Equal Employment Opportunity. It also greatly strengthened the previous laws "to enforce the constitutional right to vote."

But all three Civil Rights Acts together, from 1957 to 1964, had not made the 15th Amendment a viable part of the constitution. In some areas Negroes were still being registered to vote one by one, by the painfully slow process of individual court suits, each of which took months to prepare, with government attorneys having to prove over and over again that the law was being violated.

Unfairly applied literacy tests were still the major weapon of those who denied Negroes the vote, but there were many other devices that hostile white registrars could use if they were determined to evade or delay the law. Even when restraining orders were obtained it was difficult to enforce them.

State election officials often were uncooperative, judges sometimes unfriendly. There were long-contested court challenges, open and subtle intimidation, violence and threats of economic reprisal, warnings to blacks that if they tried to vote they might lose jobs, mortgaged farm equipment, licenses, loans, food and welfare payments.

The civil rights acts had brought some real progress, especially in Florida, Tennessee, Texas and in parts of other states where there was voluntary compliance with the laws. Not all the South remained hostile to Negro voting rights. By 1964 Negro registration throughout the eleven Southern states had grown to an estimated 2,174,000, about forty-three percent of those of voting age.

Yet there were still almost three million eligible Negroes in the South who had not been registered. The government had concentrated on the "hard core" resistance in parts of Alabama, Louisiana and Mississippi. In all the fifty counties where the Department of Justice had brought suits against registration officials, the total effort of federal protection had added only about 36,000 names to the registration lists.

In those areas and some others, the civil rights acts had done little to change local political habits. Three presidents had given the laws forceful support, and four attorneys general and their special assistants had tried to carry them out, with the backing of congress, trained legal staffs, and millions of dollars of federal funds. But none of it had really opened the vote to Negroes where local officials were determined not to let them vote. After seven years of effort only twenty-three percent of Alabama's Negroes were registered, only thirty-two percent in Louisiana, and in Mississippi still less than seven percent.

The Civil Rights Commission repeatedly had recommended direct federal intervention by an act of congress in states where officials stubbornly resisted granting voting rights. The Commission asked the federal government to send its own registrars into those states to take over the registration of qualified Negro citizens and to suspend literacy tests and other devices being used to evade the civil rights laws and the constitution.

President Johnson, in his State of the Union message on January 4, 1965, declared the time had come to "eliminate every remaining obstacle to the right and the opportunity to vote," and Attorney General Nicholas Katzenbach already was at work on the president's proposed new voting rights law, with the cooperation of Senate leaders of both political parties.

Behind it there was a stronger force, the demand of the Negro people themselves for the freedom to vote that soon would become the demand of the nation as television brought the conscience-searing drama and emotion of protest directly into the living rooms of American homes.

By the start of 1965 there were demonstrations in cities North and South, and in the park directly across from the gates of the White House. But the eyes of millions of Americans were on the little town of Selma, Alabama, where they saw for themselves, by television, what happened when Negro citizens in the "black belt" of the Deep South sought to vote.

14

SELMA, the county seat of Dallas County, Alabama, had been chosen by the Reverend Martin Luther King, head of the Southern Christian Leadership Conference, as a place that symbolized white resistance to Negro voting. He hoped a protest there would demonstrate the failure of existing laws and dramatize the need for more direct federal protection.

Dallas County's blacks had long tried to become voters but still were not allowed to vote in any number. The first voter discrimination case had been brought there back in the Kennedy administration but by 1965, despite constant litigation, the whole slow process of court action under the civil rights laws had yielded a registration of only 383 Negroes in the entire county.

When Dr. King and some of his staff moved into a previously all-white hotel in Selma on January 18, 1965, he was punched and kicked in the hotel lobby by a white segregationist. Sixty-two Negroes were arrested the next day by Sheriff James Clark and his deputies because they re- refused to use an alley entrance to the county courthouse while attempting to register as voters, and the day after that, the sheriff arrested another one hundred and fifty voter registration applicants on charges of "unlawful assembly."

By the first of February more than three thousand persons had been arrested during the Selma registration drive, including Dr. King, who spent four days in jail before posting bond for his release. As the arrests continued he announced a march from Selma to the state capital at Montgomery to protest the denial of voting rights.

The first attempt to carry it out was made on March 7, 1965, by about five hundred Negroes. As the nation watched by television, two hundred state troopers and sheriff's possemen confronted the marchers in Selma, halted them, and then charged into them with nightsticks, whips and tear gas. Seventeen marchers were so seriously injured they were taken to hospitals and altogether more than eighty were hurt or suffered from the tear gas.

In Washington, President Johnson said he was certain that "Americans everywhere join in deploring the brutality with which a number of Negro citizens of Alabama were treated when they sought to dramatize their deep and sincere interest in attaining the precious right to vote."

There were fresh protest demonstrations across the country and hundreds of Northern white sympathizers and civil rights workers, including many clergymen, went to Selma to join in the voting rights crusade. Three white ministers were attacked and beaten. One of them, the Reverend James Reeb of Boston, died of his injuries.

A second attempt to march to Montgomery, by fifteen hundred black and white demonstrators led by Dr. King, was halted in Selma after the marchers had moved only a short distance. Again confronted by state troopers, they kept their pledge of non-violence, stopped, prayed, and turned back.

On March 15, 1965, President Johnson spoke to a televised joint session of both houses of congress that met at night while, as he said, "outside this chamber is the outraged conscience of a nation." Stressing the urgent need for the new legislation he was about to propose, he said the "harsh fact" was that "in many places in this country men and women are kept from voting simply because they are Negroes" and that "no law we now have on the books . . . can ensure the right to vote when local officials are determined to deny it." The president said: "In Selma, as elsewhere, we seek peace. We seek order. We seek unity. But we will not accept the peace of stifled rights, the order imposed by fear, the unity that stifles protest. For peace cannot be purchased at the price of liberty."

What had happened in Selma was "part of a far larger movement which reaches into every section and state of America . . . the effort of American Negroes to secure for themselves the full blessings of American life," President Johnson told congress. "Their cause must be our cause too. Because it is not just Negroes, but really it is all of us, who must overcome the crippling legacy of bigotry and injustice." Borrowing the words of the black cry for freedom, he said, "And we shall overcome."

The next day the voting rights demonstrations that had been temporarily blocked in Selma shifted to the Alabama capital at Montgomery. Under the eyes of television's cameras, state and county police used electric cattle prods, sticks and rope lashes to break up a first demonstration that included two hundred young white protesters, mostly students from Northern colleges. But later that day parade permits were granted and additional hundreds of blacks and whites marched quietly in Montgomery with city police protection.

In Washington, with public pressure on congress for action, President Johnson's new voting rights bill was introduced in both House and Senate before the end of the week. "Unless the right to vote be secured and undenied," he said, "all other rights are insecure and subject to denial for all our citizens. The challenge of this right is a challenge to America itself."

During the more than four months the bill was moving through congress, against the obstructive tactics of a small but stubborn opposition, many changes in it were made. But its two central features were preserved: direct federal registration of Negroes where necessary, and the lifting of literacy tests and other devices of racial discrimination against voting.

The delayed march for voting freedom from Selma to Montgomery finally began on March 21, 1965, with Martin Luther King leading 3,200 black protesters and white sympathizers from all over the country along the first of the fifty-four miles to the Alabama capital. After the first day they marched in relays of three hundred men and women for the next four days, in accord with a federal court order upholding their right to demonstrate and restraining officials from interfering, harassing or threatening them.

When Governor George Wallace had said Alabama was "financially unable to bear the burden" of mobilizing its national guard to protect the marchers, President Johnson had federalized the guard and also ordered regular Army troops into the state, so that a total of nearly four thousand soldiers stood ready to protect the voting rights pilgrimage. By the time it ended on March 25 in front of Alabama's capitol building, what had started as a small band of Selma Negroes had grown to 25,000 black and white demonstrators.

On that last day, as in the beginning, the nation was shocked by an act of terrorism when Mrs. Viola Liuzzo, a white civil rights worker and mother of five children who had come from Detroit to take part in the Selma protest, was shotgunned to death by a band of men who had forced her car off the highway.

The Voting Rights Act reached the Senate floor on April 13, where it was delayed until leaders of both parties joined in shutting off debate by a motion of cloture that forced it to a vote on May 26, when it was approved 77 to 19. In the House the amended bill was bottled up for five weeks in the Rules Committee before it was forced to a vote on July 9 after three days of debate. The House passed its version 333 to 85, with thirty-three Southern Democrats and three Southern Republicans among those who voted for it. Both houses finally approved a conference report and on August 6, 1965, President Johnson signed the Voting Rights Act of 1965 into law.

"This is a victory for the freedom of the American Negro," he said. "But it is also a victory for the freedom of the American nation." Wherever it was clear that state officials still intended to discriminate, he explained, "then federal examiners will be sent in to register all eligible voters," but "if any county anywhere in this nation does not want federal intervention it need only open its polling places to all of its people."

The law suspended literacy tests and other devices as qualifications for voting in federal, state, local, general and primary elections in any state or county where less than half the voting age residents were voters or were registered to vote. In counties designated by the attorney general registration would be taken over by federal examiners appointed under civil service regulations. They would examine applicants, determine who was elegible to vote, and present those names to state or local officials who would be required to add them to the registration lists.

In the South, the Voting Rights Act applied immediately to Alabama, Georgia, Louisiana, Mississippi, South Carolina, Virginia, and forty counties of North Carolina. Within four days after it became law the first examiner offices were opened in nine counties in various parts of Alabama, Louisiana and Mississippi. They were soon followed by others in scattered counties throughout parts of the South where intervention was considered necessary. In postoffice buildings and federal courthouses, examiners started processing large groups of registration applicants. Hundreds of Southern blacks voted for the first time in their lives in the fall elections of 1966.

Despite dire predictions of major conflict there was no massive resistance to the Voting Rights Act throughout the South as a whole. There were pockets where resistance was stubborn and where federal examiners would remain, but after an initial period of court battles in which the constitutionality of the law was upheld, state and local officials generally accepted the fact of its strict enforcement and complied with it. Local registrars gave up the discriminatory tests and began accepting blacks as voters.

Within less than two years after the law was passed, by the spring of 1967, local registrars voluntarily had added an estimated 416,000 more Negro citizens to Southern voting lists, and federal examiners had added an additional 150,000 in the counties where they had been assigned. Two hundred Negroes held state, county or local offices, more than twice as many as were serving before the Voting Rights Act of 1965. Mississippi had elected its first Negro representative to the state legislature in nearly one hundred years and twenty more were elected to the legislatures of other Southern states.

By 1968 the rise was even more dramatic. Negro registration had grown to more than fifty percent of the black voting age population in every Southern state, if not in every county, with the most sensational change in Mississippi, where it had gone from 6.7 percent before the Act to 59.8 percent. In Selma, Alabama, where the march for voting freedom started, Negro registration had climbed from a few hundred to more than five thousand.

The Voting Rights Act had a profound and continuing effect on the whole political outlook in the South, but it was no panacea. General acceptance of the Negro as a voter and his own greater participation in the entire political process from the basics of party organization to seeking elective office, did not end all discrimination. In some places there were still threats of violence, economic reprisal, more subtle means of intimidation, and new devices to dilute the black vote and make it difficult for Negro candidates to get on the ballot or to be elected.

Yet by the time the law was amended and extended in 1970 its application, along with the use of the legal tools of the civil rights acts, the activity of federal agencies and the energetic voter education campaigns of private organizations, had increased registered Negro voters in the South to 3,324,000. That was a gain since before the Act of 1,160,000 new voters, which raised the total to nearly two-thirds of their voting age population.

From 1970 to 1971, in one year alone, there was a twenty-six percent jump in the number of Negroes elected to public office in the eleven Southern states. Alabama in 1971 had more black elected officials than any other state in the South and more than in any state in the country except for Michigan and New York.

Brought about by the people themselves, by all branches of the national government from the president to congress and the courts, and by the belatedly aroused conscience of a nation which was made increasingly aware that political discrimination against blacks had never been only a Southern problem, the Voting Rights Act was perhaps only a beginning of voter equality. But it was the biggest single stride toward the realization of Negro suffrage since the 15th Amendment had first put the promise of it into the Constitution of the United States.

15

THERE WAS A MAGIC formula, according to ancient superstition, for determining when a boy became a man. The mystical number 7 was multiplied by the number 3, the symbol for the Holy Trinity, and that made 21 the age of manhood.

It took root in English common law in the 11th Century when knights rode into battle in heavy suits of armor. A young man wasn't considered physically strong enough to bear the full weight of armor until he was twenty-one, so the castle lords set that as the age for becoming a knight and thus the age at which a youth became a man. Long tradition confirmed it as the legal age at which childhood ended and life as an adult began.

English settlers brought the established concept with them to the American colonies and when the first laws were written twenty-one was accepted as the minimum age for voting. From the time the nation was founded up until halfway through the 20th Century, that vestige of ancient superstition and medieval knighthood remained firmly fixed in the voting laws of all the states and nobody could vote until he was at least twenty-one.

The Founding Fathers had set no age limit in the constitution, since each state was left to determine the qualifications of its own voters. But by the time the 14th Amendment was ratified in 1868 twenty-one had become the standard age for first voters, so the writers of that amendment put it into the constitution. The 14th Amendment didn't state that anybody had to be that old to vote, but said a state was liable to lose some of its representatives in congress "when the right to vote . . . is denied to any of the male inhabitants of such State, being twenty-one years of age . . ."

The wording was part of the amendment's section intended to penalize states that discriminated against Negroes, and with the ending of the Reconstruction years that part remained unenforced. But it also was the only part of the constitution that specifically mentioned the age of voters and it cast some lingering constitutional doubt over later attempts to lower the voting age.

Even in the 1860's, however, there were some people who thought the young should be entitled to vote before they were twenty-one, especially young men in military service whose age denied them any voice in the decisions that sent them to risk their lives in war. Several Northern states considered reducing the voting age but finally rejected the idea, usually on the grounds that a young soldier's physical strength in battle and ability to obey commands did not necessarily mean he had the mature judgment required for intelligent voting. The same arguments, for and against soldiers voting, were to be heard during every war to come.

Early advocates of a younger voting age also argued, as others later would, that times were changing and that young men were growing up faster than their ancestors had. Back in 1867, Marcus Bickford urged delegates to a New York State Constitutional Convention to recognize the fact that twenty-one no longer was a valid yardstick for measuring maturity. "In this age in which we live, in this fast age," he said, speaking of 1867, "men mature both in body and mind at a great deal earlier period than formerly."

But twenty-one had always been the rule and most adult Americans strongly resisted changing it. As demands for change grew again during the First World War, some conservative politicians and newspaper editorialists warned that "radicals" were threatening to dilute the strength of democracy by seeking to put voting power into the hands of "mere children."

After 1920 when the 19th Amendment gave voting equality to women there was another brief revival of the movement for a younger voting age, but the majority of the newly-enfranchised females were as much against it as the males who finally had recognized women as citizens. Adults of both sexes showed little desire to share the ballot with sons and daughters who had not yet come of legal age.

Young people themselves helped shape the slow beginning of change in public opinion about their right to vote. During the hard years of depression many were forced to take on adult responsibilities of helping families to survive. Others actively worked in the New Deal's projects of conservation, rebuilding, reform. Young women as well as young men soon were needed even more in the booming factories of war production and in the swelling military forces as the nation faced the Second World War. Whatever the law might say, many obviously were growing up before they were twenty-one, and the question of changing the voting law became a national issue.

A public opinion poll in 1939 indicated that seventy-nine percent of America's adults were still against letting young people vote. But by the time the United States was fully engaged in World War II the opposition to a lower voting age had dropped to only forty-two percent. It was to change again, both for and against, in the years ahead. The real battle for the youth franchise finally had started but it would take more than thirty years to be won.

During the early 1940's there were attempts in many states to change the laws to let young people vote. President Franklin Roosevelt avoided any public statement that might be taken as direct presidential interference with the states although it was widely reported that his administration favored state action to lower the voting age. Mrs. Eleanor Roosevelt openly urged the change. Republican Senator Arthur Vandenburg went even further in 1941 and called for an amendment to the federal constitution that would give all Americans the right to vote at eighteen.

Democrat Jennings Randolph of West Virginia, then a young congressman, "fathered" the proposed constitutional amendment by introducing a resolution for it in the House of Representatives in 1942, which produced the first congressional hearings on the question the following year, but his bill never got beyond that. For the next twenty-eight years, as a congressman and then as a senator, Randolph went on introducing resolutions and working for passage of the amendment.

More than one hundred and fifty versions of it were introduced by various senators and representatives of both political parties in the years that followed the first proposal. The amendment was offered in one branch or the other at least once in every congress. Five times it reached the stage of committee hearings in the Senate, which helped give the idea national publicity and slowly increased congressional support, but not enough to force the amendment through.

In the states, the first crack in the solid wall against voting before the age of twenty-one came in Georgia, where Governor Ellis Arnall personally led a drive to amend his state's voting law in favor of young soldiers with a slogan of "Fight at 18, vote at 18!"

The state amendment narrowly squeezed through the legislature but was overwhelmingly approved by the people of Georgia in a referendum in August, 1943. They voted three to one to make theirs the first of the United States to allow voting for all citizens at eighteen. But for the next twelve years Georgia remained the only state where young people could vote.

With America plunged into the Korean War so soon after the end of World War II, the 18-vote gained stronger public backing in the 1950's. Opinion polls repeatedly showed that the majority of Americans favored giving young men who had to fight the wars the right to vote.

Even without a vote thousands of young people took a direct part in the presidential campaign activities of 1952. Many were attracted to politics for the first time by the idealism of Democratic candidate Adlai Stevenson and others worked equally hard at campaign offices and rallies to win presidential victory for the Republicans and war hero General Dwight Eisenhower.

Democrats, still in control of the outgoing congress, managed to get a bare quorum of the Senate Judiciary Committee to approve the proposed constitutional amendment in 1952 but a week later congress adjourned and no action was taken. Republicans, coming into power in 1953, introduced new resolutions for the amendment and once again there were committee hearings but nothing more. Half a dozen states meanwhile considered changing their own voting laws but none did and Georgia still stood alone on the side of 18-year-old voters.

President Eisenhower tried to break the congressional stalemate with the surprise decision to put the full weight of his administration behind the constitutional amendment. "For years our citizens between the ages of eighteen and twenty-one have, in times of peril, been summoned to fight for America," he said in his State of the Union message in January, 1954. "They should participate in the political process that produces this fateful summons. I urge congress to propose to the states a constitutional amendment permitting citizens to vote when they reach the age of eighteen."

Some of the leading Democrats in congress joined Republicans in immediately introducing new legislation to carry out the president's call. On March 15, 1954, the Senate Judiciary Committee approved the proposed amendment by a 7 to 3 vote, and for the first time in its history it was brought out of committee to the floor of the Senate.

Washington correspondents reported it still faced a stiff

fight. Many senators said they favored the age drop in voting, but that it was a matter for the states to decide. A newspaper survey of governors of the states showed that many of them also were against federal "interference" with the rights of the states to determine who should vote. But by then thirty-seven states had considered the 18-vote at one time or another and, with the exception of Georgia, no state had approved.

Senate Republicans were solidly behind the administration's push for the amendment but the parliamentary maneuvering of opponents finally forced a vote at the worst possible time for it. Late in the afternoon of May 21, 1954, on a Friday when many senators had left early to get away for the weekend, debate began.

State's rights quickly became the central issue, with Senator Richard Russell of Georgia, the only state with 18-year-old voters, leading the opposition that came mainly from Southern senators determined to protect their state voting laws against what they claimed was threatened federal invasion. Backers answered that women had been given the vote by constitutional amendment and that the proposed 18-vote amendment still would have to go before all the states for ratification so the states would have final decision.

After only two hours of debate, the Senate suddenly was brought to a vote, after four-thirty on the weekend Friday afternoon. The move caught thirty-seven of the Senate's members not there, including some of the amendment's strongest supporters. All the Republicans still in the chamber, along with seven Democrats, voted for it, a total of thirty-four votes in favor. But there were twenty-four Democrats against it, fourteen of them from the South. By five votes short of the required two-thirds majority, the proposed amendment failed. It would be another seventeen years before the Senate voted on it again.

There was a second small break in the ranks of the states in 1955 when Kentucky decided to join Georgia and let its 18-year-old citizens vote. When the new states of Hawaii and Alaska later entered the Union they also had lower voting ages, twenty in Hawaii and nineteen in Alaska. But except in those four states voters everywhere still had to be at least twenty-one.

16

As in every struggle by the people to expand their voting rights, the real power for change in the minimum voting age had to come from the people themselves, and it came finally from the young people of the 1960's.

They grew up faster than any generation had before, in an age when nothing seemed impossible for man to do, not even reaching for the moon by the exploration of space, but also an age of violence and shock that opened their minds to a deep questioning of the goals man ought to be reaching for. Shut out of the political system by denial of the vote, they became the most politically and socially active young generation America had yet seen.

Many grew to youth from a childhood fed on an over-abundance of material promises offered on the wishing box of television. But as television's children they also had seen discrimination, rural poverty, and the desperation of the ghetto. They felt deeply for those Americans who were ill-fed, poorly-schooled, untrained for jobs, and deprived of opportunity. They saw the pollutions of the environment, the corruption of laws, the misuses of power.

As no people at home had ever done before, they saw for

themselves the horror of war spread over Vietnam, in vividly shown detail that became an every-night picture of the battlefield killing, the bombings, burnings. Every day they heard the televised promises of the men in Washington that there would be quick victory and an end to war. And the war grew bigger and the talk went on and the meaning went out of it but nobody stopped the killing. They knew that many of them would be drafted to kill or be killed, without any say of their own, and for no good reason.

At the start of the decade they had been inspired by President John Kennedy's call to "ask not what your country can do for you but what you can do for your country," and they saw him assassinated. They shared Martin Luther King's dream of an America where people someday would "not be judged by the color of their skin but by the content of their character," and they saw Martin King murdered. In Senator Robert Kennedy many of the young found hope again for a man they wanted for president, and they saw him shot to death.

They had shown their concern for a better America by working in countless youth groups advocating social change. They had infused the civil rights movement with their determination and with a courage often needed to face physical danger. With no voting right of their own, they had crusaded for the voting rights of others, and had helped to register thousands of blacks to vote.

When there seemed no other way to force attention on all the wrongs they saw, they took to protests and demonstrations on the campuses and in the streets. Sometimes, in frustration or in provocation, the demonstrations were lost to violence and destruction, to the outrage of the whole meaning of democracy, and the many who protested peacefully were blamed for the terrorizing acts of a radical minority that deliberately sought confrontation.

Admonished to work for change within the established political system that had locked them out, thousands did in the elections of 1968. In spring primary campaigns voteless young Americans dedicated themselves to getting out the voters for candidates pledged to end the war and to correct social evils. They aroused the leaders of both parties, liberals and conservatives, to a new awareness of youth's potential power to change the old ways of politics as usual in the United States.

Hundreds went into New Hampshire before the nation's first primary there in March to work for Minnesota's Senator Eugene McCarthy. He had come out of nowhere as a presidential candidate to challenge the greatest vote-getter in history, his own party's incumbent President Lyndon Johnson, at that time the obvious choice of the Democrats for renomination. To McCarthy's young supporters the choice was between peace or continuing war and not since the civil rights marches in Mississippi had so many young Americans committed themselves so fervently to a cause.

Newspapers at first treated the seemingly hopeless campaign as something of a joke and made fun of the fact that some young men working for McCarthy cut their long hair and shaved off beards and that some girls traded short skirts for dresses less likely to shock New Hampshire's farmers. But the young McCarthy backers worked eighteen hours a day getting out campaign literature, checking voter registration lists name by name, traveling through the still-

frozen countryside from village to farm, ringing every door-
bell, talking to voters about the war.

In that single effort, they all but pulled the political rug
out from under the President of the United States. They
changed the whole concept of the coming national election. McCarthy scored so heavily in the March primary
that he came within a few hundred votes of capturing New
Hampshire's Democratic nomination. Lyndon Johnson, instead of being a sure-thing candidate, became a candidate
who faced a loss of voter confidence and disruption in his
party, and by his own decision soon was not a candidate
at all. He announced in April that he would not run again.

Some of the young battled through other primaries for
McCarthy, with mixed results, and some others cam-
paigned for Robert Kennedy and cheered him through to
victory in the California primary, and on the eve of that
victory saw him killed. Still, young people crowded into
Chicago when the Democratic National Convention was
held, hoping by anti-war demonstrations that they could
force the party to their views.

Among them were some who had lost faith in orderly
democratic process and who called for the complete disruption of the convention, violent confrontation, revolution.
They were a mixture of sincere protesters and those who
came with more radical intentions. Chicago became an
armed camp, with police standing off the demonstrators
while the convention met behind barbed-wire barricades
where security protection was harshly enforced.

Inside the convention hall delegates clashed in furious
debate that all but tore the Democratic party apart over
the war and over the organization's nomination of Vice-

President Hubert Humphrey as the presidential candidate. Outside in the streets of Chicago there was riot as an army of police turned in force against demonstrators and by-standers. There were clubbings, beatings, screams of fear and rage, and a long aftermath of national shock in which some Americans bitterly condemned police and party boss-ism and others praised the maintenance of law and order.

Youth could claim no victory in Chicago but if many who went there left in complete disillusion with all polit-ical involvement because of what had happened, the fact remained that, praised or denounced, the young had made their political presence felt.

Like every age group, not all the young thought the same way about anything, and not all were Democrats. Many young people were as active in campaigning for Richard Nixon, previously nominated by a Republican party united behind him, and for other Republican candidates. And the great majority of the young were not political or campus activists of any kind.

About half of all those between the ages of eighteen and twenty-one were already married and many had taken on the responsibility of raising families. Millions were working at full-time jobs in farms, factories and offices, and others had part-time work that included them among the ranks of taxpaying citizens.

By the laws of many states they were given and accepted full adult responsibility at eighteen for operating automo-biles, owning guns, entering into legal contracts, making wills, taking out insurance policies, and were held account-able for their actions by criminal courts. They could marry without consent, become heads of households, work at any job without restriction, enter the federal civil service system, and were old enough to be conscripted into the armed forces.

They were not only the best-educated younger generation in history but better educated than any older age group in the population. More than eight out of ten had graduated from high school by the age of eighteen, as compared with only five who had finished high school in 1940, and more than half of them were seeking higher education. Physically they were more mature, intellectually they were better-equipped, and the communications revolution had made them better-informed about national issues than those their age had been in the past. But they could not vote.

President Johnson had suggested in a special message to congress in 1968 that the voting age be lowered. The Democratic party, at the youth-beleaguered Chicago convention, had written into its platform a pledge to support "a constitutional amendment lowering the voting age to eighteen." Democratic presidential candidate Humphrey spoke in favor of it.

The Republican party platform, while it did not endorse a constitutional amendment, called on the states individually "to re-evaluate their positions with respect to 18-year-olds voting." Republican presidential candidate Nixon many times during his campaign repeated the call for action by the states. "The reason the voting age should be lowered is not that 18-year-olds are old enough to fight," he said. "It is because they are smart enough to vote. . . . Youth today is just not as young as it used to be. This watershed political year of 1968 has shown us that young people need not be of voting age to have a real impact. . ."

Under the chairmanship of Senator Birch Bayh of Indiana, who had fought for the 18-vote as an assemblyman in his own state years before he came to Washington, the Senate Subcommittee on Constitutional Amendments held extensive hearings in the spring of 1968 to explore the whole question again. Those who testified represented a broad range of political views and were almost unanimous in saying the time had come to extend the franchise to the young.

In congress, however, the amendment still lacked the support to bring it to a vote. That was before the convention turmoil in Chicago, before the elections, and before youth had made its political influence so strongly felt.

As street and campus demonstrations continued to spread in 1969 the investigating National Commission on the Causes and Prevention of Violence, headed by Dr. Milton Eisenhower, called for a reordering of the nation's priorities and strongly advocated, among other things, the constitutional amendment to change the voting age.

"Many of the young people in the nation today," the Commission reported, "are highly motivated by the ideals of justice, equality, candor, peace—fundamental values which their intellectual and spiritual heritage has taught them to honor. . . . Moreover, they speak eloquently and passionately of the gap between the ideals we preach and the many social injustices remaining to be corrected. . . . A combination of high ideals, tremendous energy, impatience at the rate of progress, and the lack of constructive means for effecting change has led some of today's youth into disruptive and at times violent tactics for translating ideals into reality." It went on:

"The nation cannot afford to ignore lawlessness. . . . It is no less permissible for our nation to ignore the legitimate needs and desires of the young. . . . The anachronistic voting age limitation tends to alienate them from systematic political processes and to drive them into a search for alternative, sometimes violent, means to express their frustrations over the gap between the nation's ideals and actions. Lowering the voting age will not eliminate protest by the young. But it will provide them with a direct, constructive, and democratic channel for making their views felt and for giving them a reasonable stake in the future of the nation."

President Nixon, by early 1970, had come to the decision that the constitutional amendment was the best way to grant 18-year-olds the vote. It was with a new sense of urgency for immediate action on it that the Senate Subcommittee on Constitutional Amendments took up its hearings again in February, 1970.

"Can we, in good conscience, expect youth to work within the system when we deny them that very opportunity?" asked Chairman Bayh, as he began the hearings in a committeeroom crowded with young people. "The contradiction is too great. It should not survive. It will not survive. And that is why we are here today."

Senator Jennings Randolph, who had introduced the proposed amendment twenty-eight years before and had battled for it since, announced to the subcommittee that the new resolution he had introduced already had the pledged votes of seventy senators, more than the two-thirds majority needed to pass it in the Senate.

"In our 193-year history we have worked to expand the base of the democratic processes in our country. Full participation is the ideal for which men and women have been striving through the years," Randolph said. "The future in large part belongs to young people. It is imperative that they have the opportunity to help set the course for that future."

Senator Edward Kennedy of Massachusetts said that lowering the voting age was "the most important single principle we can pursue as a nation if we are to succeed in bringing our youth into full and lasting participation in our institutions of democratic government."

Educators, psychologists and other scientists testified to the increased maturity of modern youth. Legal experts pointed to the fact that the laws treated 18-year-olds as adults in almost everything but voting rights. Statements of support for the amendment came from officials of some twenty national organizations of teachers, lawyers, minority and civil rights groups.

Senator Barry Goldwater of Arizona, the Republican presidential candidate of 1964, called the idealism of youth "exactly what we need more of in this country. . . . more citizens who are concerned enough to pose high social and moral goals for the nation" because "civil servants and legislators of any political party need to be prodded to cut through the bureaucratic jungle of redtape so that government will serve the people the way it is intended." There was "no sensible reason for denying the vote to the 18-year-olds," he said. "What's more, I think we have studied the issue long enough. The voting age should be lowered and lowered at once across the entire nation."

But despite strong subcommittee report for the proposed amendment there were roadblacks in its way. The full Judiciary Committee was reluctant to hurry it to the Senate floor for a vote. In the House, where for almost three decades since the amendment was first proposed it had never reached even the level of full committee hearings, more delay seemed certain.

The most serious obstacle of all, as things stood in early 1970, was the necessary ratification by three-fourths of the states, since the states had consistently rejected all attempts to change their own laws to allow voting at eighteen. There were gloomy predictions that ratification of the proposed amendment might mean a state-by-state battle that could go on for years.

Thousands of young people had been actively at work in the states trying to change the voting laws. They had held rallies, petitioned, lobbied for hearings and political support, testified before committees, struggled to get legislatures to consider the question, sought referendums, planned election strategy, organized, raised funds, and carried their campaigning to the people.

Backing their campaigns on a state and national level was the Youth Franchise Coalition of more than thirty political, educational, youth and social work organizations, most of which also had extensive programs of their own to mobilize and organize students, teachers and the general public behind state drives for the 18-vote. But since 1966 voters in eight states had rejected the youth vote, no large state had yet given the approval that might have encouraged others to follow, and there had just been two major defeats, in Ohio and New Jersey in November, 1969.

To many it seemed unlikely that states which had refused to change their own voting laws would be eager to ratify an amendment by which the federal government would change those laws for them. With the groundswell of feeling against some students because of campus disorders, political columnists were saying there was little chance an amendment would get through congress and the states in time for any 18-year-olds to cast presidential ballots before 1976 at the earliest, if the amendment ever was ratified by the states at all.

17

Senator edward kennedy of Massachusetts took the lead in suggesting a way to avoid the whole slow and cumbersome method of constitutional amendment. Convinced that congress had authority under the 14th Amendment to give young people the vote by passing a law to do that, instead of by amending the constitution, Kennedy and his research staff carefully prepared the legal groundwork. While the Senate hearings on the proposed 18-vote amendment were still underway, he produced his substitute plan for a direct act of congress.

The Democratic floor leader of the Senate, Mike Mansfield of Montana, long a champion of the 18-vote, also thought the time had come for direct action to avoid the lengthy and uncertain process of amending the constitution. With shrewd political strategy he moved to add the 18-vote as a rider to the Voting Rights Act of 1970, already under debate in the Senate, so the two would be mutually dependent and each would strengthen the other.

By adding it to another bill which was under urgent consideration, it would avoid risking the 18-year-old vote as a separate measure. It would tie them so tightly together that both houses of congress and even the president eventually would have to accept or reject the whole package Mansfield made.

The basic Voting Rights Act of 1970, which had been approved by the House before being sent to the Senate, extended for another five years the expiring 1965 act that protected Negro voter rights in the South. The Senate version also put a nationwide ban on literacy tests and established uniform thirty-day residency requirements for voting in presidential elections. What Mansfield added was an amendment to the Voting Rights Act reducing the voting age to eighteen in all federal, state and local elections after January 1, 1971, by the declaration of congress.

It was the finding of congress, it said, that "the requirement that a citizen be twenty-one years of age as a precondition to voting . . . . denies and abridges the inherent constitutional rights of citizens eighteen years of age but not yet twenty-one years of age . . . (and) has the effect of denying . . . the due process and equal protection of the laws that are guaranteed to them under the Fourteenth Amendment to the Constitution."

Therefore congress found it "necessary to prohibit the denial of the right to vote" to any otherwise qualified citizen "on account of age if such citizen is eighteen years of age or older."

Senate spokesmen for the Nixon administration fought it on the grounds that congress would be exceeding its constitutional authority. They and others also strongly objected to the procedure of tying two highly controversial proposals together instead of presenting them as separate measures. But after three days of debate the Senate adopted the Mansfield amendment to the Voting Rights Act on March 12, 1970, by an overwhelming vote of 64 to 17. The following day the Senate passed the entire amended package and returned it to the House for final action.

President Nixon personally intervened in an attempt to block it by writing a public letter to Speaker John McCormack and House leaders, saying he favored the 18-vote and also favored the Voting Rights bill but that "these are entirely separate issues." He called for the youth franchise by constitutional amendment and warned that if the House approved the Senate rider it was likely to be declared unconstitutional with "immense and possibly disastrous effects."

Senator Kennedy answered by accusing the president of asking congress "to abdicate our function of interpreting the Constitution and carrying out its mandate." Kennedy said: "We know that the Voting Rights Act is the only realistic hope of achieving the goal of bringing our youth into the mainstream of the political process in America. To counsel delay when success is at last within our grasp is to counsel defeat and generate intolerable new frustrations for millions of young Americans."

Early in June, 1970, the House Rules Committee cleared the bill after opponents had failed in an attempt to send it to a joint conference of the House and Senate in the hope of knocking out the voting age provisions. Approval by the committee meant the combined measure would not be subject to amendment by the House, which would have to vote for all of it or none. The rules also limited the total time of debate on it to one hour, half an hour for each

side, even though the 18-vote had never in its history been
debated at all in the House.

The House galleries were crowded with anxious young
people when the limited debate began on June 17. Speaker
McCormack, soon to retire, made a rare personal appear-
ance on the floor to speak for the voting act, saying that
if it were adopted this would be the "happiest day" of his
long career in congress. He and others argued that without
it 18-year-olds might be kept from voting for years.

Leading the opposition, Republican minority leader Ger-
ald Ford warned of grave consequences for the nation if
young people were allowed to vote in elections and afterwards the act was declared unconstitutional. Even if congress did pass it, he questioned whether President Nixon
could "in good conscience" sign it.

Before the final vote the act came to a test on a motion
that might have opened the way to send it back to committee. The bill cleared the test, with fifty-nine Republicans joining the majority of Democrats who voted for it,
and the young people in the galleries broke into cheering
and applause. Some congressmen on the floor applauded
too, and Speaker McCormack made no attempt to pound
his gavel and quiet the demonstration. When the final
vote came, the House approved the Senate-amended voting
act 272 to 132 and sent it to the president.

President Nixon spent five days deciding whether to veto
it, but finally signed it saying "if I were to veto, I would
have to veto the entire bill," in a statement explaining his
dilemma. He had to sign or else veto the basic provisions of
the Voting Rights Act that had struck down racial barriers
to Negro voting in the South.

But he signed despite what he called "my misgivings" about the other part of the act that lowered the voting age. "Although I strongly favor the 18-year-old vote," he said, "I believe . . . that Congress has no power to enact it by simple statute but rather it requires a constitutional amendment."

The president emphasized his opinion by signing without ceremony, in a private White House office without spectators and with only an aide as a witness, and used his own fountain pen instead of the souvenir pens that are usually given out after historic documents are signed.

"I have directed the Attorney General to cooperate fully in expediting a swift court test," he said. "Because of the likelihood that the 18-year-old vote provisions of this law will not survive its court test, the constitutional amendment pending before the Congress should go forward to the states."

The new law was brought to its swift test before the Supreme Court that bypassed the lower courts. Four suits finally were consolidated to determine all the major issues, two of the suits brought by states to invalidate the law and two by the Department of Justice to uphold it.

The Department of Justice had to defend the constitutionality of a law it had advised congress would be unconstitutional. Attorney General John Mitchell, who had signed the government's written briefs in favor of the law, was the close advisor of the president who had made it a law while publicly doubting its constitutionality.

Because of that relationship, Mitchell decided not to defend the law personally when the Court heard oral arguments on October 19, 1970. Solicitor General Erwin Gris-

wold was the only lawyer who argued for it and five lawyers representing various states argued against it. The Justices asked very few questions, but Justice Hugo Black did
briefly question one of the attorneys about the effect of
the law if it were restricted only to federal elections, a
point considered of minor importance at the time.

On December 21, the Supreme Court made its decision
that opened the door to legal voting by more than eleven
million young Americans. It opened it only part-way, by
saying they could vote in federal elections but not state
and local elections, but that was far enough to create the
final pressures of public opinion that would bring them all
the way to their full right to vote.

The Supreme Court's ruling in favor of the 18-year-old
vote in federal elections rested upon the opinion of 84-year-
old Justice Black. Four justices considered the voting age
provision entirely constitutional for both federal and state
elections and four other justices believed it was entirely
unconstitutional in any elections. Justice Black sided partly
with one group and partly with the other.

He held that the authority of congress under the 14th
Amendment to overrule the voting standards of the states
applied only when the states discriminated on the basis of
race and that therefore congress acted unconstitutionally
when it lowered the voting age for state and local elections.

On the other hand, it was also his opinion that under
the First Article of the constitution, dealing with the times,
places and manner of holding elections, congress had "ultimate supervisory power" over congressional and presidential elections. Although no other justice joined in his opinion, Justice Black cast the deciding vote between the
divided groups and it was declared the judgment of the

Court that young people could vote in federal but not in state and local elections.

The Court ruling threatened to throw the election systems of forty-seven states into confusion. All the states that had never allowed young citizens to vote faced the possibility of having to establish two separate systems of registration and voting, one for those who could now start to vote at eighteen in presidential and congressional elections and another for those who couldn't vote until an older age in state and local elections.

The administrative problems of creating and maintaining dual-age voting would call for the hiring of hundreds of additional state and municipal employees. It would mean spending millions of dollars to purchase extra voting machines or to change old machines, or to print separate paper ballots, election forms and records. Dual-voting would lead to delay at the polls and in counting returns and would multiply all the chances of disputed elections, errors and fraud.

Besides, to many of the older generation as well as to young people themselves, it was obviously unfair to say that a person was old enough to help run the nation but too young to know about things closest to home. Since there was no longer any question about whether young citizens would be allowed to vote in some elections, most Americans saw no logic in disrupting the whole election system instead of letting them vote in all elections the way everybody else did.

There was a sudden rush in many states to try to change their own voting laws in a hurry and end the confusion by setting a minimum age of eighteen for all elections. But in most states that would require a state constitutional amendment, arrived at by the slow process of legislative action, referendum and ratification by the voters.

At the same time, with more pressure from the people than ever before, the demand grew for an amendment to the federal constitution that would set a uniform voting age in all the states at once. The right of 18-year-olds to vote by act of congress, followed by the Supreme Court decision, finally had made the long-debated and delayed amendment not just a possibility but a national desire and a public need.

Congress made the proposed 26th Amendment its first important business in 1971. The outpouring of letters and telegrams, the ringing of telephones in congressional offices, and the appeals from worried state officials put such urgency behind it that seldom has any amendment gone through congress with more speed and less opposition.

Only once since the first resolution for the amendment was introduced in 1942 had it gotten out of committee in 1954 to debate on the Senate floor after which it was defeated. But when it came to a vote in the Senate in March 10, 1971, not a single senator voted against it. Senate approval was by a vote of 94 to 0.

Less than two weeks later, on March 23, it came to a vote in the House. Representative Emanuel Celler of New York, guided it through, as he previously had guided through the three constitutional amendments before it, the 23rd, 24th and 25th. "By offering this amendment," the 82-year-old dean of the House said, "perhaps I can again wear the robes of youth."

During the House debate some representatives argued that instead of extending the youth franchise congress should repeal the act that allowed 18-year-old voting in federal elections. But there was only token opposition and the debate was brief. When the vote was taken, the House gave the proposed amendment the final approval needed from congress by an overwhelming 400 to 19 and sent it to the states for ratification.

Minnesota's legislature, waiting for the news to be telephoned from Washington, acted within minutes after congress approved and became the first state to ratify. Within hours three other states, Connecticut, Tennessee and the state of Washington, ratified without waiting for formal notification.

Newspapers had been predicting that full ratification by the necessary thirty-eight states would take at least a year and probably longer. But the predictions were wrong. Almost all opposition to voting by young people had collapsed. The states raced the amendment through the final ratification in only a little more than three months after it began, which was far faster than any amendment to the constitution had ever been ratified before.

Wednesday morning, June 30, 1971, Alabama became the thirty-sixth state to ratify. That afternoon North Carolina took its final action and became the thirty-seventh. That night Ohio's state House of Representatives met and gave its assent, and the 26th Amendment became part of the Constitution of the United States, with its guarantee that:

"The right of citizens of the United States who are eighteen years of age or older to vote shall not be denied or abridged by the United States or by any state on account of age."

Some Other Books
About the Right to Vote

General

Claude, Richard, *The Supreme Court and the Electoral Process*, The Johns Hopkins Press, Baltimore, 1970.

McGovney, Dudley, *The American Suffrage Medley*, University of Chicago Press, Chicago, 1949.

Porter, Kirk, *Suffrage in the United States*, University of Chicago Press, Chicago, 1918.

Williamson, Chilton, *American Suffrage from Property to Democracy*, Princeton University Press, Princeton, N.J., 1960.

Secret Ballot

Albright, Spencer, *The American Ballot*, American Council on Public Affairs, Washington, D.C., 1942.

Fredman, L. E., *The Australian Ballot: The Story of American Reform*, Michigan State University Press, 1968.

Presidential Election

Peirce, Neal, *The People's President*, Simon & Schuster, New York, 1968.

Wilmerding, Lucius, *The Electoral College*, Rutgers University Press, New Brunswick, N.J., 1958.

Direct Vote For Senators

Haynes, George H., *The Senate of the United States: Its History and Practice*, Vol. I., Houghton Mifflin Co., Boston, 1938.
————, *The Election of Senators*, Henry Holt & Co., New York, 1906.
Rienow, Robert and Leona, *Of Snuff, Sin and the Senate*, Follett Publishing Co., Chicago, 1965.

Woman Suffrage

Flexner, Eleanor, *Century of Struggle*, Harvard University Press, Cambridge, Mass., 1959.
Severn, Bill, *Free But Not Equal: How Women Won the Right to Vote*, Julian Messner, New York, 1967.

Negro Voting Rights

U.S. Commission on Civil Rights, *Political Participation*, 1968 Report, CR1.2:P 75/3, U.S. Government Printing Office, Washington, D.C., 1968.
————, *The Voting Rights Act: The First Months*, CR 1.2: V.94/2, U.S. Government Printing Office, Washington, D.C., 1965.

18-Year-Old Vote

Subcommittee on Constitutional Amendments of Committee on Judiciary, U.S. Senate, *Lowering the Voting Age to 18*, February, 1971, Report, U.S. Government Printing Office, Washington, D.C., 1971.
————, *Hearings Relating to Proposed Constitutional Amendments Lowering the Voting Age*, February–March, 1970, U.S. Government Printing Office, Washington, D.C., 1970.

Index